JARDIN DU LUXEMBOURG

The perfect Paris[...]
park. See page[...]

[...] to the world's most [...] page 36.

MONTMARTRE

Artistic heritage, lively bars and some of the most romantic streets in the city. See page 63.

PLACE DES VOSGES

One of Paris' most lovely squares. See page 52.

NOTRE-DAME

A monument to Catholicism and the skill of the great Gothic architects. See page 28.

MUSÉE D'ORSAY

A treasure trove of Impressionist works. See page 76.

A PERFECT DAY

8.00am

Breakfast
If your hotel doesn't serve breakfast, ask the concierge for directions to the nearest good *boulangerie*; buy some freshly-baked croissants or *pains au chocolat* and find a leafy square nearby to eat them in.

11.00am

Coffee break
At the Palais du Luxembourg, turn left and walk along the railings of the famous Jardin du Luxembourg, the most elegant of Paris parks. Stop for a strong espresso at smart café Le Rostand (see page 114), on the square at the garden's eastern tip.

9.00am

Seine boat tour
Begin at the city's origin, the River Seine. Make your way to the western tip of the Île de la Cité, via the steps down from Pont-Neuf. From here, take one of the Vedettes du Pont-Neuf boat tours; it is a lovely way to see the city.

10.30am

Rue de Seine
From Pont-Neuf, walk along quai de Conti, then amble down characterful rue de Seine with its art and fashion boutiques.

12 noon

Park and lunch
After a stroll through the Jardin du Luxembourg among joggers, *boules* players and smooching couples, make your way to nearby restaurant La Ferrandaise (see page 114) and enjoy a nice light lunch of updated French classics.

4.30pm

Retail therapy

Make your way back to Métro St-Paul and go straight to Charles-de-Gaulle-Étoile station. Take a moment outside the station to admire the Arc de Triomphe (see page 57), then walk down the Champs-Élysées, dipping into the swanky, big-brand shops as you go.

9.30pm

Bar hopping

Walk downhill to boulevard de Roche-chouart and take a taxi to the République and Oberkampf area, which is littered with trendy bars. Try rue Jean-Pierre Timbaud, which runs parallel to rue Oberkampf, just east of place de la République – the perfect counterpoint to the historic attractions you saw earlier.

2.00pm

Paris history

Walk towards the river along teeming boulevard St-Michel, then catch the Métro to St-Paul. Walk up rue Malher to the Musée Carnavalet (see page 51) and spend an hour or two exploring Paris' history through the paintings and artefacts.

6.00pm

Montmartre and dinner

Take the Métro to Abbesses, on the hill of Montmartre. Follow your nose through the atmospheric, winding streets. After a relaxed bistro dinner at Chez Toinette (see page 112), walk to Sacré-Cœur and savour the panoramic view over the city from its front steps.

CONTENTS

Walking Eye App

...download of the ...ow from the free ...gle Play. Simply ...e eBook dedicated ... information on ...during your stay, ...ontent for a wide ...ase in-app.

HOW TO DOWNLOAD THE WALKING EYE APP

Available on purchase of this guide only.
1. Visit our website: www.insightguides.com/walkingeye
2. Download the Walking Eye container app to your smartphone (this will give you access to your free eBook and the ability to purchase other products)
3. Select the scanning module in the Walking Eye container app
4. Scan the QR Code on this page – you will be asked to enter a verification word from the book as proof of purchase
5. Download your free eBook* for travel information on the go

* Other destination apps and eBooks are available for purchase separately or are free with the purchase of the Insight Guide book

INTRODUCTION

It's hard to argue with Victor Hugo's description of Paris as 'the city of cities'. For over 2,000 years, it has steadily grown in size and reputation, and each of its many layers is rich in history and intrigue. Unlike many European cities, it was left almost unscathed by the two world wars, and its celebrated streets, monuments and museums still work their centuries-old magic today. And then there's the artistic heritage of the 'City of Light'; long a powerhouse of art, literature, music and philosophy. Little wonder that the Parisians are so proud to be part of a city that, according to writer Jean Giraudoux, has been home to 'the greatest amount of thinking, talking and writing in the world'.

GEOGRAPHY

Paris is where all the French channels of communication lead; it is the beating heart of the country. From its core, the 20 Parisian *arrondissements* (administrative districts) spiral out like a snail's shell, a pattern that reflects the city's historical development and successive enlargements.

Paris centers around the River Seine, whose flowing waters have long been the lifeblood of the city. The River Seine enters Paris close to the Bois de Vincennes in the southeast and meanders gently north and south past three small, heavily developed islands – the Île St-Louis, Île de la Cité and, on its way out, Île des Cygnes. Chains of hillocks add perspective to the city, with Montmartre (the city's highest point), Ménilmontant, Belleville and

Culture capital

Despite concerted attempts at decentralisation in France, Paris continues to dominate the country's art and literature, music, fashion, education, scientific research, commerce and politics.

Buttes Chaumont rising up to the north of the river, and to the south, Montsouris, the Mont Ste-Geneviève, Buttes aux Cailles and Maison Blanche.

Paris is notionally contained by the Périphérique; a ring road of 35km (22 miles). Built in 1973 to reduce traffic jams, the Périphérique is now invariably congested itself. With 1.1 million cars using the road's 34 exits each day, its future is currently being discussed. Forming two concentric rings wrapped tightly around Paris, the suburbs (known, sometimes derisively, as *la banlieue*) are divided up into *départements*, or counties, much as the rest of France.

At the beginning of the 19th century, Napoleon imposed a special status on the city of Paris, giving it the powers of a *département* in order to maintain a firm hold on the capital's politics and populace. Today, each *arrondissement* also has its own council and mayor to deal with local affairs. In the two houses of the French Parliament, 21 delegates and 12 senators represent the city.

THE RIVER

Fluctuat nec mergitur ('Buffeted by the waves but does not sink'), reads the Latin inscription on the capital's coat-of-arms, symbolising a city born beside the River Seine. The city takes its name from the old Gallic tribe of the Parisii who, according to Julius Caesar, sited their chief city on the largest island in the river. However, the city did not divide the river for long; Roman Lutetia was later founded on the left bank of the Seine in the modern day Latin Quarter area. Today, the Seine cuts a swathe through the city's middle. The Seine is the capital's widest avenue, spanned by a total of 37 bridges, which provide some of the loveliest views of Paris.

The river is the city's calmest thoroughfare, notwithstanding the daily flow of tourist and commercial boat traffic. In the 19th century, the banks were encumbered with wash-houses and watermills, and its waters heaved with ships from every corner of France. More difficult to imagine are the 700 Viking warships that sailed up the river to invade Paris in the 9th century, or the thousands of bodies that floated past in 1572, victims of the St Bartholomew's Day Massacre, turning the Seine into a river of blood. Today, barges and pleasure boats ply the river, some on their way to Burgundy via the St-Martin and St-Denis canals, which cut across the northeast of the city.

PARIS AMBIENCE

One of the most persistent images of Paris is one of long avenues elegantly lined with chestnut and plane trees. Flowers and plants abound in a patchwork of squares, parks and gardens, tended in the formal French tradition, or following the

Paris rooftops

English style so admired by Napoleon III. Divided up by two long ribbons of streets, one tracing a long line north to south (from boulevard de Strasbourg to boulevard St-Michel) and the other running from east to west (from rue du Faubourg-St-Antoine as far as La Défense), Paris is a mosaic of *quartiers* (quarters) or 'villages', each with a distinctive character. Chains of boulevards encircle the city centre, marking its medieval boundaries. Several streets contain the word *faubourg*, indicating that they were once part of the suburb outside the city wall.

The most important, unofficial division in Paris is between the traditionally working-class eastern end of the city and the mostly bourgeois west. In general, the further east you go, the further left you will find yourself on the political spectrum. Rents are steep in the western *arrondissements*, whereas

CAFÉ CULTURE

Cafés have long played a key part in the city's intellectual, political and artistic development. Café Voltaire (1 place de l'Odéon) was where, in the 18th century, Voltaire used to meet fellow philosopher Diderot to discuss their Enlightenment theories. The 19th-century poets Verlaine and Mallarmé also conversed here, and in the 1920s the American writers Ernest Hemingway and F. Scott Fitzgerald extolled the café's 'sudden provincial quality'. Between the two world wars, other writers in Paris spent hours at their favourite tables in Le Procope (13 rue de l'Ancienne-Comédie), while the Existentialist writer and philosopher Jean-Paul Sartre and his lover Simone de Beauvoir consolidated the highbrow reputation of Les Deux Magots (6 place St-Germain-des-Prés) in the 1950s. The Art Deco Café de Flore (172 boulevard St-Germain) was another *intello* favourite. Today, politicians congregate at Brasserie Lipp across the road.

property is less expensive, though hardly affordable, in the east. City planners have been struggling for decades to improve the balance, culminating in massive urban renewal projects at Bercy and the 'new' Left Bank (see page 74) in the southeast.

POPULATION

Paris is more densely populated than Tokyo, London or New York. At odds with the spacious boulevards, Parisians live literally on top of

Legendary Left-Bank Café de Flore

one another, squeezed into small apartments, packed into the city's 100 sq km (40 sq miles). A house or a garden are almost unheard-of luxuries. There is intense competition for desirable living space, with an average of 150,000 people looking for a home at any one time. It is an oft-cited paradox that this battle for a place to live occurs in a city where 16 percent of apartments lie vacant. Soaring house prices since the 2000s have left many landlords happy to sit on vacant investments. High rents can mean that many Parisians have neither the time nor the money to appreciate the city they live in, being trapped in a monotonous routine they describe as *Métro-boulot-dodo* (commuting, working, sleeping).

Nonetheless, for anyone fortunate enough to live in the city centre, the rewards far outweigh the demands. Human in scale, clean, safe, cosmopolitan and lively, Paris lives up to its reputation as one of the best cities on earth for enjoying the good life.

A BRIEF HISTORY

Paris began as an island fishing community and trading port in the middle of the River Seine. Stone Age inhabitants left some of the earliest traces (4500BC) on the Right Bank under what is now Bercy, but it was *c.*250BC before the town took form under the skilful hands of the Parisii. According to the Greek geographer Strabo, the Celtic tribe built their main city on the largest island on the river, presumably the Île de la Cité. The island, well away from the banks of the river – much wider than today – may well have provided refuge from the fierce Belgae to the east. The Parisii minted their own finely crafted gold coins for trade as far afield as Britain and the Mediterranean, and the town's prosperity and strategic position attracted the attention of Julius Caesar, whose legions conquered it in 52BC.

Clovis, King of the Franks

According to some philologists, the town's Gallo-Roman name of Lutetia means 'marshland', reflecting the character of the land that then bordered the river. The Romans built their settlement just above the flood plain, on what is now the Left Bank's Latin Quarter. Rue St-Jacques and rue St-Martin follow the route of the old Roman road linking northern France to Orléans. Scant subterranean masonry has been found from the Roman buildings – forum, theatres, temples – but there are substantial remains of the public baths in what is now a wing of the Musée National du Moyen Age.

Huns and Franks overran Roman Gaul in the 3rd century, driving the citizens to retrench in the fortified Île de la Cité, which was renamed Paris around this time. In 508, Clovis, King of the Franks, set up court here. He later converted to Christianity, and several religious foundations date from this time, including those of the city's oldest church, St-Germain-des-Prés.

Places of worship

France has no official state religion, but the sway of the Catholic church during the nation's long history is still very much in evidence. As well as its many Catholic churches, Paris has a long list of places of worship dedicated to other varieties of Christianity and other faiths, notably Judaism, Islam and Hinduism.

THE CAPETIANS

Norman pirates regularly raided Paris from AD 845 onwards. The city stagnated until 987, when Hugues Capet, Count of Paris, became King of France. His Capetian dynasty went on to make the city the economic and political capital of France. The River Seine was once again the key to commercial prosperity, symbolised by the ship on the city's coat-of-arms. The Right Bank port area, known as the Grève, developed around the site of the present-day Hôtel de Ville.

Philippe Auguste (1180–1223) used the revenue from trade to build the Louvre fortress (its lower ramparts are clearly visible beneath today's museum), Notre-Dame Cathedral, paved streets, aqueducts and freshwater fountains. To protect his investment while he was away on the Third Crusade, he surrounded the city with walls.

The profoundly devout, and later canonised, Louis IX (1226–70) gave the city one of its great Gothic masterpieces,

Sainte-Chapelle. His patronage of spiritual and intellectual life also gave rise to the learned character of the modern day Latin Quarter. The Sorbonne university evolved from the many new schools established here, frequented in their day by Latin-speaking clerics and established by the king's chaplain, Robert de Sorbon. By the end of Louis's reign, Paris was one of the largest cities in Western Christendom, with a population of 100,000.

In the 14th century, the city's merchant class took advantage of the political vacuum left by the devastating Black Death and the Hundred Years War with England. In 1356, with King Jean le Bon held prisoner at Poitiers, Etienne Marcel – the merchants' leader – set up a municipal government in Paris. Although he was assassinated two years later, he had shown that the Parisians were a force to be reckoned with. Wary of their militancy, Jean's successor Charles V built the formidable Bastille fortress.

ENGLISH RULE AND RELIGIOUS CONFLICT

Civil unrest continued unabated. In 1407 – during the second phase of the Hundred Years War between England and France – the Duke of Burgundy had the Duke of Orléans asassinated on rue Barbette, which led to 12 years of strife between their supporters. The Burgundians allied themselves with the English, who entered Paris in 1420, following the French defeat at Agincourt under Henry V, the English King. Henry had just signed the Treaty of Troyes with King Charles VII of France, which made him Regent and his son, Henry VI, King of England and France, at nine months old. Charles VII retained vast territories in central and southern France and, ten years after Troyes, Joan of Arc was able to lead the French army to several important victories in France, while England was divided by its nobles' interests. The Treaty of Arras (1435) between Charles VII and Henry's former ally, Philip III of Burgundy, brought the dual monarchy to an end. Charles VII reclaimed Paris in 1436 and by 1453, the English Monarchy had lost all its possessions in France, save Calais.

In the early 16th century, Paris thrived under an absolutist and absent monarch, François I (1515–47), who was occupied with wars in Italy, and even imprisoned for a year in Spain. Much of the Louvre was torn down and

Henri IV's Place des Vosges

rebuilt along the present lines. A new Hôtel de Ville (city hall) was begun, as well as the grand St-Eustache church.

The new splendour was soon bloodied by religious war, starting in 1572 with the St Bartholomew's Day massacre of 3,000 Protestants in Paris and culminating in the siege of the city by Henri de Navarre in 1589. Before the Catholic League capitulated, 13,000 Parisians had died of starvation. Henri was crowned at Chartres and finally entered the capital in 1594 – not before having converted to Catholicism himself, though his quip 'Paris is well worth a Mass' is almost certainly apocryphal.

Henri IV did Paris proud once he was its master. He built the beautiful place des Vosges and place Dauphine, embellished the banks of the river with the quai de l'Arsenal, quai de l'Horloge and quai des Orfèvres, and even constructed the Samaritaine hydraulic machine that pumped fresh water to Right Bank households until 1813. The most popular of France's monarchs, *le bon roi Henri* (good King Henry) was a notorious ladies' man. He completed the Pont-Neuf (the oldest bridge in Paris), as well as the adjacent gardens, where he was known to dally with his ladies.

Louis XVI faces the guillotine

During the reign of Louis XIII (1610–43), Paris began to take on the fashionable aspect that became its hallmark. Elegant houses sprang up along rue du Faubourg-St-Honoré, and the magnificent *hôtels* (mansions) of the nobility were constructed in the Marais. The capital strengthened its hold on the country with the founding of a royal printing press and Cardinal Richelieu's Académie Française.

Paris increasingly attracted nobles from the provinces – although too many for the liking of Louis XIV, *le Roi Soleil* ('the Sun King', 1643–1715). To bring his overly powerful and independent aristocrats into line, Louis decided to move the court out to Versailles, compelling the courtiers to live at ruinous expense in his enormous new palace.

Paris lost some of its political importance, but looked more impressive than ever, with the landscaping of the Jardin des Tuileries and the Champs-Élysées, and the building of the Louvre's great colonnade and the Invalides hospital for wounded soldiers. The city asserted a leading cultural position in Europe with its new academies of the arts, literature and sciences and the establishment of the Comédie Française (1680) and several other theatres. By this time, the population had increased to 560,000.

The rumble of popular discontent grew louder however, as corruption and heavy taxes for costly foreign wars marked the reigns of the Sun King's successors, the languid Louis XV

(1715–74) and the inept Louis XVI (1774–93). One of the final construction projects of the *ancien régime* was a 23km (14 mile) wall encircling the city. Begun in 1784, it was a key factor in the subsequent unrest, for at points along the wall taxes were collected on goods brought into the city.

THE REVOLUTION

Paris was the epicentre of the political earthquake that was the French Revolution, whose aftershocks spread across France to shake up a whole continent. It started with protests about taxes, but turned into an assault on the privileges of the monarchy, the aristocracy and the church. Middle-class intellectuals made common cause with the urban poor, the previously powerless *sans-culottes* (literally, people without breeches). The revolutionaries destroyed the prison-fortress of the Bastille on 14 July 1789, and proceeded to execute the perceived enemies of the new republic.

A climax was reached on 21 January 1793, with the public beheading of Louis XVI. In the Reign of Terror later that year, several revolutionaries followed Louis to the guillotine: Camille Desmoulins, the fiery orator; Danton, who tried to moderate the Terror; and then the men who had organised it, Robespierre and Saint-Just.

FIRST EMPIRE

In 1799, Napoleon Bonaparte became first consul, and later made himself emperor. For Paris, he performed all the functions of an enthusiastic mayor, scarcely hindered by his military expeditions abroad. In Moscow, for instance, he found time to draw up statutes for the Comédie Française. Detailed maps of Paris and architectural plans for new buildings were always part of his baggage. For all his spectacular monuments – the Arc de Triomphe is one example – the emperor was proudest

> ### Guillotine bridge
>
> Masonry from the Bastille was used to build the bridge leading to what was then the place de la Révolution – now place de la Concorde – where the guillotine was erected.

of his civic improvements: better fresh water supplies, improved drainage, new food markets and a streamlined municipal administration and police force. Most of his reforms survived long after his final defeat in 1815.

THE RESTORATION

Although the monarchy was restored in 1814, it faced an ever-present threat in Paris from dissatisfied workers, radical intellectuals and a highly ambitious bourgeoisie. In July 1830 protest turned to riots and the building of barricades. Charles X was forced to abdicate. However, instead of restoring the republic, the revolutionary leaders played it safe and accepted the moderate Louis-Philippe, the so-called 'Citizen King'.

The Revolution of 1848, which brought Louis-Philippe's monarchy to an end, likewise started with riots and barricades in the streets of Paris. A mob threatened the royal palace, forcing the king to flee; they then invaded the Chamber of Deputies, demanding a republic. Elections followed, but they showed that however radical Paris might be, the rest of France was still largely conservative. The new National Assembly withdrew the concessions that had been made to the workers, and up went the barricades again. This time the army was called in with its heavy guns. At least 1,500 insurrectionists were killed, and thousands deported.

SECOND EMPIRE

The democratically elected president, Louis-Napoleon (a nephew of Napoleon Bonaparte, whose son had died young), seized absolute power in 1851 and the following year became

Emperor Napoleon III. Fear led him to modernise Paris. The insurrections of 1830 and 1848 had flared up in the densely populated working-class districts around the centre, and he wanted to prevent a recurrence. He commissioned Baron Georges Haussmann to do away with the narrow and insalubrious alleys that nurtured discontent, and moved the occupants to the suburbs. The city was opened up with broad avenues; these so-called *grands boulevards* were too wide for barricades and gave the artillery a clear line of fire in case of revolt.

The Second Empire was a time of joyous abandon and expansion, but the emperor stumbled into war against Prussia in 1870. The army was quickly defeated, and Napoleon III's disgrace and capture brought the proclamation of a new republic, followed by a crippling Prussian siege of Paris. The city held out, albeit reduced to starvation level. When France's leaders agreed to peace, there was another uprising.

THIRD AND FOURTH REPUBLICS

The Paris Commune, the surprisingly moderate and efficient rule of an elected revolutionary council, lasted 10 weeks, from 18 March to 29 May 1871, until Adolphe Thiers, the first president of the Third Republic, sent in troops from Versailles to crush it. In the last days, the *communards* set fire to the Palais des Tuileries and executed hostages. At least 20,000 Commune supporters were executed in retaliation.

Napoleon Bonaparte

Prosperity rapidly returned, marked by a great construction boom. Projects begun under Napoleon III, such as

General Charles de Gaulle

the Palais-Garnier and the huge Les Halles market, were finished. The city showed off its new face at the 1889 World Fair, with the Eiffel Tower as its monumental centrepiece. The splendid Métro system was inaugurated in 1900.

After this period of peace, however, two wars took their toll. The Germans failed to take Paris during World War I, but occupied it for four years (1940–44) during World War II. The city escaped large-scale bombing, and Hitler's vengeful order to destroy the city before retreating was ignored. Liberation came eventually, with a grand parade down the Champs-Élysées by General Charles de Gaulle, his Free French forces and US and British allies.

The post-war city regained its cultural lustre under the influence of figures such as Camus, Sartre, Juliette Gréco and be-bop musicians. Under a rapid succession of governments, however, economic recovery was slow.

FIFTH REPUBLIC

The Fourth Republic collapsed in 1958 after an army revolt during the colonial war in Algeria. Recalled from retirement, de Gaulle became the first president of the Fifth Republic and set about the task of restoring French prestige and morale.

FROM THE 1968 RIOTS TO MITTERRAND'S PRESIDENCY

Barricades and insurrection hit Paris again in May 1968. With workers on strike, students hurled the Latin Quarter's paving stones at the Establishment. However, national elections showed that Paris was once more at odds with most of France, which voted for stability. Succeeding de Gaulle, Georges Pompidou affirmed the new prosperity with controversial riverside expressways and skyscrapers, and the striking Beaubourg cultural centre that bears his name.

In 1977 Jacques Chirac became the first democratically elected mayor of Paris in over a century. At a time when politicians could double as mayor and prime minister, Parisians benefited from leaders who furthered their national political ambitions with a dynamic municipal performance. Although many questioned his taste in the shopping mall that replaced the old markets of Les Halles, Chirac is credited with the effective clean-up of the formerly dirty streets.

President François Mitterrand (1981–95) made his mark on the Paris skyline with a series of imposing works (his *grands projets*): the pyramid centrepiece of the reorganised Louvre, the Grande Arche de La Défense, the Opéra Bastille, the Institut du Monde Arabe and the national library that bears his name.

FAMILY VALUES

France's birthrate of 2.03 children per family exceeds the European average, but is still a source of concern for the state. Every *famille nombreuse* (families with three children or more) is rewarded with benefits including nursery provision, subsidised public transport, car tax and school meals, as well as free admission to museums. The current population of France is around 65.8 million, higher than that of the UK (at 63.7 million). The birthrate has been boosted by France's large Muslim community, whose numbers are, according to many demographers, steadily rising.

PARIS TODAY

Chirac became president in 1995. However, within two years his popularity had dwindled, and the Socialist leader Lionel Jospin became prime minister. Their period of joint stewardship was one of economic growth, reduced unemployment and rising property values. In 2001 Bertrand Delanoë became the city's first Socialist mayor for 130 years (and was re-elected seven years later). Although Chirac beat the National Front candidate Jean-Marie Le Pen in the 2002 presidential election, the huge support for Le Pen shocked the world. In his second term, President Chirac led a determined opposition to the war in Iraq, which saw his ratings soar, only to plummet after initiating reforms to the state pension and benefit system. His party's candidate to succeed him, Nicolas Sarkozy, won the presidency in May 2007 with promises of sweeping economic and social reforms. His 'Grand Paris' scheme, which aimed to make the city and its suburbs a single administrative unit, has seen improved transport links and the construction of landmark skyscrapers. However, he alienated French voters with his high-handed style and fondness for luxury; so much so that in 2012 François Hollande became the first Socialist president since François Mitterrand. In April 2014, Anne Hidalgo was elected the first female mayor.

François Hollande

In January 2015, 12 people were killed and 11 injured in an attack by Muslim extremists on the Paris headquarters of the *Charlie Hebdo* satirical magazine. Following the shooting, hundreds of thousands of people participated in marches against terrorism.

HISTORICAL LANDMARKS

c.250 BC Celtic settlement in the Paris area.

52 BC Roman conquest and founding of Lutetia on the Left Bank.

508 Clovis, King of the Franks, makes Paris his capital.

987 Hugues Capet elected King of France.

1431 Henry VI of England crowned King of France.

1436 English expelled.

1594 Henri IV enters Paris.

1682 Louis XIV moves court to Versailles.

1789 Storming of Bastille starts French Revolution.

1793 Execution of Louis XVI and Marie-Antoinette; Reign of Terror.

1804 Napoleon Bonaparte becomes emperor.

1814–15 Fall of Napoleon; restoration of Bourbon monarchy.

1830 Bourgeois revolution; Louis-Philippe, the Citizen King.

1848 Revolution brings Louis-Napoleon to power.

1870–1 Franco-Prussian War; Second Empire ends; Paris besieged.

1871 Paris Commune – 10 weeks of workers' rule.

1900 First Métro line opened.

1914–18 World War I. Germans advance to within eight miles of Paris.

1939 World War II begins.

1940 French government capitulates; Germans occupy Paris.

1944 Free French and other Allied forces liberate Paris.

1958 Fall of Fourth Republic. De Gaulle becomes president.

1968 Student riots, workers' general strikes.

1977 Jacques Chirac becomes first elected mayor since 1871.

1981 President Mitterrand elected president.

1995 Jacques Chirac elected president.

2002 The euro replaces the franc as France's unit of currency.

2007 Nicolas Sarkozy elected president.

2012 Socialist François Hollande elected president.

2014 Paris elects its first female mayor, Anne Hidalgo of the Socialist Party.

2015 Twelve people are killed and 11 injured in a January terrorist attack by Muslim extremists on the Paris headquarters of *Charlie Hebdo* magazine.

WHERE TO GO

Paris is a compact and logically ordered city that anyone can quickly get the hang of. Its public transport networks are highly efficient, but by far the best way to get to know the city is to potter around it on foot, allowing plenty of time for aimless but often fruitful digressions. The river creates the main division, and the Right Bank (Rive Droite) and Left Bank (Rive Gauche) have their distinct, long-established associations. Right has the reputation as the powerhouse of business and commerce; Left is the historic centre of learning. There is also a traditional east-west divide between the wealthy west and poorer, more radical east. But even these boundaries are porous, and arty centres of creativity are now more likely to be in the northeast of the city than in affluent St-Germain-des-Prés, and young urban professionals are increasingly buying into the traditionally working class parts of the city.

Administratively, the city is divided into 20 *arrondissements*, starting with the 1st in the centre (taking in Île de la Cité and the area around the Louvre) and spiralling outwards clockwise to end at the 20th in the northeast. Confusingly, while Parisians often refer to the *arrondissement* in which they live, they also refer to the historic *quartiers,* such as the Marais, Bastille or Latin Quarter, that often straddle *arrondissements* (the Marais, for example, extends into the 3rd and the 4th *arrondissements*; the Latin Quarter into the 5th and 6th).

ÎLE DE LA CITÉ

The Île de la Cité has long been the heart of Paris. During the 3rd century BC, the Celtic Parisii tribe are thought to have set up home on this, the largest island in the Seine. In 52BC, Roman legions conquered the settlement and founded

Place de la Concorde and the Eiffel Tower

Métro sign

Lutetia Parisiorum on the left bank. During the Middle Ages, the island was the centre of political, religious and judicial power, not only for Paris but for the whole of France. Nowadays, the island is still the geographical centre of the capital and home to several of the city's main official buildings. Sainte-Chapelle and Notre-Dame make the island an enduring focus for religious tourism.

NOTRE-DAME

Dominating the island is **Notre-Dame ❶** (www.notredamede paris.fr; Mon–Fri 8am–6.45pm, Sat–Sun 8am–7.15pm; visits restricted during services). The site has played a religious role for at least 2,000 years. In Roman times a temple to Jupiter stood here; in the 4th century AD it was replaced by a Christian church, St-Etienne; this was joined two centuries later by a second church, dedicated to the Virgin. Norman raids left them both in a sorry state, and, in the 12th century, Bishop Maurice de Sully decided that a cathedral should be built to replace them.

The main part of Notre-Dame, begun in 1163, took 167 years to finish. Its transition from Romanesque to Gothic has been called a perfect representation of medieval architecture – an opinion that has provoked some dissent. Cistercian monks protested that such a sumptuous structure was an insult to the godly virtue of poverty, and today some architectural purists still find Notre-Dame excessive.

The original architect is unknown, but Pierre de Montreuil (who was involved in the building of Sainte-Chapelle, see page 32) was responsible for much of the 13th-century work. The present look of the cathedral is due to Eugène Viollet-le-Duc, who from 1845 to 1863 restored it to repair the ravages of the 18th century, caused more by pre-Revolutionary meddlers than by revolutionaries stripping it of religious symbols. Popular support for the expensive restoration was inspired by Victor Hugo's novel, *Notre-Dame de Paris*.

The cathedral has witnessed numerous momentous occasions over the centuries, including, in 1239, the procession of Louis IX, during which the pious king walked barefoot, carrying his holy treasure – believed to be Christ's crown of thorns. In 1594 Henri IV made his politically motivated conversion to Catholicism here to reinforce his hold on the French throne. Napoleon

Notre-Dame and the eastern end of the Île de la Cité

Climb up Notre-Dame's towers for great views of the city

crowned himself emperor at Notre-Dame, upstaging the Pope, who had come to Paris expecting to do it; the scene is depicted in Jacques-Louis David's vast painting, *The Consecration of Napoleon,* now in the Louvre. Other occasions include General de Gaulle marking the 1944 Liberation of Paris with a Mass here, and in 1970 his death was also commemorated here.

THE WEST FRONT

Across the three doorways of the west front, the 28 statues of the **Galerie des Rois** represent the kings of Judah. These are 19th-century restorations: the originals were torn down during the Revolution because they were thought to depict kings of France. Twenty-one of them were discovered in 1977 and moved to the Musée du Moyen Age (see page 69).

The central **rose window** depicts the Redemption after the Fall. Two more outsized rose windows illuminate the transept; the northern one retains most of its 13th-century glass. A 14th-century *Virgin and Child* is to the right of the choir entrance.

The 255-step climb up the **north tower** (www.monuments-nationaux.fr; daily Apr–Sept 10am–6.30pm, Oct–Mar 10am–5.30pm, until 11pm weekends July–Aug; charge) is rewarded with glorious views of Paris and close-ups of the roof and Notre-Dame's famous gargoyles. Cross over to the south tower to see the 17th-century 13-ton tenor bell, Emmanuel, which was joined by a new tenor bell, Marie, in 2013; eight new bells were installed in the north tower at the same time. There are spectacular views from here too. Napoleon III's town planner Baron Haussmann greatly enlarged the *parvis*, or cathedral forecourt, increasing the impact of the towering west front. Excavations beneath the square have revealed walls and foundations from the Gallic, Roman and medieval eras, which now form part of an exhibition on early Paris. A copper marker set into the ground, known as the Kilomètre Zéro, is the point from which all distances from Paris to the rest of France are measured.

PALAIS DE LA CITÉ

The other architectural and historical highlight on the Île de la Cité is the **Palais de la Cité**, the complex of buildings that includes the Conciergerie, Sainte-Chapelle and the Palais de Justice, the headquarters of the French supreme court.

Notre-Dame's magnificent Rose Window

War memorial

Behind Notre-Dame is the Mémorial des Martyrs de la Déportation (Tue–Sun Apr–Sept 10am–7pm, Oct–Mar until 5pm; free), a poignant memorial dedicated to the 200,000 French deported to concentration camps during World War II.

PALAIS DE JUSTICE

The imposing neoclassical **Palais de Justice** (www.ca-paris.justice.fr; Mon–Fri 8.30am–6pm; free), heart of the French legal system, stands on the site of the Roman palace where Emperor Julian was crowned in AD 360. The lobby (Salle des Pas Perdus) is well worth a visit to catch a glimpse of the lawyers, plaintiffs, witnesses, court reporters and hangers-on.

THE CONCIERGERIE

Adjacent is the **Conciergerie** ❷ (www.monuments-nation aux.fr; daily 9.30am–6pm; charge), which became a state prison in 1370. The 'medieval' facade is misleading; it dates from the 1850s. The building's greatest notoriety dates from the late 18th century: in 1793, at the height of the Terror, the Conciergerie became the antechamber of the guillotine, with around 2,500 prisoners spending their last night here (see page 19). It is now a museum to its bloody past, displaying items including a guillotine blade, the crucifix before which Marie-Antoinette prayed while captive here, and the lock used on Robespierre's cell. Look out on the Cour des Femmes, where husbands, wives and lovers were allowed a final tryst before the tumbrels came to carry off the prisoners.

SAINTE-CHAPELLE

Concealed in the courtyard between the Palais de Justice and the Conciergerie is the magnificent Gothic **Sainte-Chapelle** ❸ (www.monuments-nationaux.fr; daily Mar–Oct 9.30am–6pm, Nov–Feb 9am–5pmt charge). The chapel was constructed in 1248 to designs by Pierre de Montreuil to house holy relics, fragments of which were believed to be Christ's Crown of Thorns, bought by the pious King Louis IX (later St-Louis). The lower chapel, with its star-patterned ceiling, was used by palace servants. More impressive is the upper level, where light blazes through 15m (45ft) high glass windows separated by buttresses so slim that there seems to be no wall at all. Of the 1,134 individual pieces of glass, 720 are 13th-century originals.

Between 1789 and 1815 Sainte-Chapelle served various roles: as a flour warehouse in the Revolution, as a club for high-ranking dandies, then as an archive for Napoleon's Consulate. This latter role fortunately saved the chapel from projected destruction,

Exquisite stained-glass in Sainte-Chapelle

since the bureaucrats could not think of another site in which to keep their mountains of paper.

OTHER ATTRACTIONS ON THE ÎLE DE LA CITÉ

Towards the western end of the island is the pretty, tree-shaded **square du Vert-Galant** and, beyond it, a statue of Henri IV and the restored **Pont-Neuf**, which, despite its name – 'New Bridge' – is the oldest bridge in Paris. The bridge owes its survival to its solid stone – rather than wood – construction, and it was the first bridge in Paris to be constructed without houses on it. In 1985, the Pont-Neuf hit the headlines when Bulgarian-born American artist Christo wrapped the entire structure in fabric.

At the eastern end of the island is the colourful **Marché aux Fleurs** on place Louis Lépine, opposite the Préfecture de Police and Hôtel Dieu. The latter, now a hospital, was built on the site of a medieval hospital; it was the scene of intense battles when the police rose up against the occupying Germans in 1944. In contrast to these forbidding structures, the market is an array of small glasshouses selling flowers and plants. On Sunday, the stalls become a market for caged birds.

ÎLE ST-LOUIS

The pedestrianised Pont St-Louis crosses from the Île de la Cité to the **Île St-Louis ❹**, an island renowned for its elegant, exclusive and astronomically expensive mansions. From the western end of the shady quai d'Orléans (at the western end of the island) there is a wonderful view of the apse of Notre-Dame. However, some pilgrims to this spot are more intent on a visit to another Parisian institution: ice-cream parlour **Berthillon** (Wed–Sun 10am–8pm), at 29–31 rue St-Louis-en-l'Île, the street that cuts through the island. It is a pretty road, dotted with boutiques and restaurants. Towards the eastern end is the baroque church of **St-Louis-en-l'Île** (Mon–Sat

Elegant and exclusive Île St-Louis

9.30am–1pm, 2–7.30pm, Sun until 7pm), notable for its fine collection of Dutch, Flemish and Italian 16th and 17th century art.

On the northeastern end of the island, at 17 quai d'Anjou, is the grand **Hôtel Lauzun**. Built in 1640 by Louis Le Vau, architect to Louis XIV, it is now owned by the City of Paris. It was here that the poets Théophile Gautier and Charles Baudelaire lived in 1845, and where Baudelaire wrote part of *Les Fleurs du Mal*. In the **Hôtel Lambert**, on the corner of rue St-Louis-en-l'Île, Voltaire enjoyed a tempestuous love affair with the lady of the house, the Marquise du Châtelet.

On the island's south bank is the small **Musée Adam Mickiewicz** (by reservation only Thu 2.15–5.45pm, tel: 01 55 42 83 88; charge). A Polish poet, Mickiewicz (1798–1855) lived in Paris from 1832 to 1840 and devoted himself to helping oppressed Poles. The 17th century building in which the museum is housed also includes the Polish Library and displays memorabilia of the Polish composer Frédéric Chopin.

THE LOUVRE, TUILERIES & CONCORDE

PALAIS DU LOUVRE

The Louvre was eight centuries in the making, but has retained great architectural harmony nonetheless. It was originally built as a fortress by Philippe Auguste in 1190. When Louis XIV moved his court to Versailles, he abandoned the Louvre to artists and other squatters. The Revolutionaries made it a public museum in 1793. As the home of the *Mona Lisa,* the Louvre drew almost unmanageable crowds, until President Mitterrand ordered its reorganisation in the 1980s. A vast reception area and main entrance was excavated in the forecourt and topped by the iconic glass **Pyramid** designed by Sino-American architect I.M. Pei.

MUSÉE DU LOUVRE

The **Musée du Louvre** ❺ (tel: 01 40 20 53 17; www.louvre.fr; Wed–Mon 9am–6pm, Wed and Fri until 9.45pm, tickets valid all day and allow re-entry into the museum; charge; free first Sunday of the month) is divided into three wings: Richelieu in

MAKING THE MOST OF THE MUSEUMS

Entry charges for museums range from around €5–12, with reduced rates for children, students and pensioners. Some museums charge less on Sundays, and entrance is always free on the first Sunday of the month for the following: the Louvre, Musée d'Orsay, Centre Pompidou, Musée de l'Orangerie, Musée Rodin, Musée Picasso and Musée du Moyen Age. **The Paris Museum Pass** (www.parismuseum pass.com) gives entry to over 60 museums and monuments in Paris and its surroundings, including the Louvre and Versailles. You can buy passes valid for two, four or six consecutive days at museums, tourist offices and Métro stations.

The Louvre is a masterpiece of symmetry

the north, Sully in the east and Denon in the south. The collections are arranged in colour-coded sections. A free map is available at the ticket desks, while the useful official mobile app can also be downloaded free.

The following is a summary of the Louvre's many treasures, including some of the highlights in the different sections.

LOWER-GROUND AND GROUND FLOORS

A good place to start is the exhibition on the medieval Louvre, on the lower-ground floor of the Sully Wing. This is where you can see the remains of Philippe-Auguste's fort and keep, and some of the artefacts discovered in the 1980s excavations. On the lower ground floor of the Denon Wing is the Department of Islamic Art, which opened in 2012 and is recognisable by its iridescent, undulating roof. Above, on the ground floor of the Sully Wing, are Egyptian and Greek Antiquities, and on the ground floor of the Denon wing are Etruscan and Roman antiquities.

The lower ground floor of the Richelieu wing showcases French sculpture, including Guillaume Coustou's giant *Horses of Marly*. The French sculpture collection continues on the ground floor of the Richelieu wing, with works spanning the 5th to 18th centuries. Also here are Mesopotamian finds, such as the black basalt Babylonian *Code of Hammurabi* (1792–1750BC), one of the world's first legal documents.

FIRST AND SECOND FLOORS

The first floor houses some of the biggest crowd-pullers. The first floor of the Denon Wing is a spectacular collection of large-format French painting, notably Delacroix's *Liberty Leading the People*, Géricault's *Raft of the Medusa* and David's *Consecration of Napoleon*. Adjacent is a room showcasing Leonardo da Vinci's enigmatic Florentine noblewoman, the *Mona Lisa* (known in

Inside the Louvre

French as *La Joconde*). This iconic piece, painted in 1503, is now displayed behind bulletproof glass in a special, frequently crowded room that it shares with Veronese's vast *Wedding at Cana* canvas.

Leonardo's Mona Lisa

At the staircase dividing the Denon and Sully wings is the *Winged Victory of Samothrace* (2nd century BC), a Hellenistic figurehead commemorating a victory at sea, and the glittering Galerie d'Apollon (Apollo's Gallery), home to the crown jewels. At this point you reach the Sully Wing and the graceful Hellenic statue of the *Venus de Milo* (2nd century BC), bought by the French government for 6,000 francs in 1820 from the island of Milos. Most of the first floor of the Richelieu Wing houses works of the decorative arts.

The whole second floor is dedicated to painting, with highlights including Dürer's *Self-Portrait*, Vermeer's *The Lacemaker*, Watteau's *Pierrot* and Ingres's *The Turkish Bath*. The Richelieu Wing houses works from Flanders, the Netherlands, Germany and France (14th to 17th centuries); the second floor of the Sully Wing is devoted to French paintings of the 17th, 18th and 19th centuries.

ADDITIONAL MUSEUMS

In a separate wing are three other collections (107 rue de Rivoli; www.lesartsdecoratifs.fr; Tue–Sun 11am–6pm, Thu until 9pm; charge). The **Musée des Arts Décoratifs** presents a survey of interior design, from medieval tapestries to 21st-century design. The **Musée des Arts de la Mode et du Textile**

Arcades of the Palais-Royal

covers Paris fashions and textiles from the 16th century to the present day. Upstairs, the **Musée de la Publicité** is home to a rich collection of advertising from the Middle Ages to the present.

PALAIS-ROYAL

The **Palais-Royal** ❻ is directly north of the Louvre, across rue de Rivoli. Built in 1639 as Cardinal Richelieu's residence, it gained its regal title when Anne of Austria moved in with young Louis XIV. This serene, arcaded palace has a colourful past. In the days of Philippe d'Orléans, Prince Regent while Louis XV was a child, it was the scene of notorious orgies. A later duke (another Philippe) built apartments above the arcades, along with two theatres (one now the Comédie Française, see page 96), shops, gambling houses and fashionable cafés.

Despite efforts to curry favour with the revolutionaries, such as calling himself Philippe Égalité (equality), the duke ended up on the guillotine with the rest of the family. After the Revolution, the palace became a gambling den again and narrowly escaped destruction during the 1871 uprising. However, following the restoration of the monarchy (1872–76), it regained respectability. The palace now houses the Ministry of Culture, the Council of State, the Constitutional Council, some shops and the historic Grand Véfour restaurant (see page 108).

East of the Palais-Royal is the **Banque de France**, and immediately north is the **Bibliothèque Nationale Richelieu** (www.bnf.fr; Mon–Fri 10am–6pm, Sat until 5pm; free). The latter became a royal library in 1368, when Charles V placed 973 manuscripts in the Louvre. Most of the millions of books, engravings and ancient manuscripts it has accumulated over the centuries have been transferred to the newer national library on the Left Bank (see page 74). The old building with its splendid reading room (1863) has been transformed into a specialist research library.

THE TUILERIES

West of the Louvre is one of the city centre's main green spaces, the **Jardin des Tuileries** ❼ (daily Apr–May 7am–9pm, June–Aug until 11pm, Sept–Mar 7.30am–7.30pm; free), commissioned in 1564 by Catherine de Medici to be the garden for her new Palais des Tuileries. The tuileries were workshops that made roof tiles here, before the crown purchased the site and André Le Nôtre landscaped the area. The Tuileries Palace was the formal home of the French monarchy until its destruction in the upheaval of the Paris Commune in 1871. The current gardens extend across the palace's former site.

Walk around the chestnut and lime trees, and admire sculptor Aristide Maillol's sensual statues of nymphs and languorous maidens, a few of which are coquettishly concealed behind a miniature maze. A project, due to be completed in 2020, is currently underway to restore the gardens to their original glory and to make them even more welcoming to the 14 million people who visit them each year.

Cour d'Honneur

In 1986, artist Daniel Buren installed rows of black-and-white-striped stone columns in the Palais-Royal's main quadrangle, the Cour d'Honneur.

Claude Monet's Water Lilies

At the eastern entrance to the Tuileries is the pink **Arc de Triomphe du Carrousel,** built by Napoleon at roughly the same time as the Arc de Triomphe. The latter is visible from here in a straight line beyond the Obelisk on place de la Concorde. The same axis continues into the distant haze to the skyscrapers of La Défense.

JEU DE PAUME AND MUSÉE DE L'ORANGERIE

A few surviving fragments of the Palais des Tuileries can be seen by the **Jeu de Paume,** in the northwest corner of the gardens. Once home to real-tennis courts (hence the name) and later to the collection of Impressionist paintings now displayed at the Musée d'Orsay, the building is currently the attractive showcase for the **Centre National de la Photographie** (www.jeudepaume.org; Tue11am–9pm, Wed–Sun until 7pm; charge). The centre showcases changing exhibitions on all photographic disciplines, including major fashion retrospectives and contemporary video installations.

In the southwest corner of the Tuileries is the **Musée de l'Orangerie** (www.musee-orangerie.fr; Wed–Mon 9am–6pm; charge). The building was originally constructed by Napoleon III to shelter the orange trees of the Jardin des Tuileries, but since the 1920s has been the showcase for eight of Claude Monet's water-lily paintings, the Nymphéas series. In these works, the Impressionist painter captured the play of colour on the pond in his Japanese garden at Giverny (see page 88) at different times of day. Monet and the Louvre's architect drafted the original plans and elevations for their display at the museum. Extensively renovated and reopened in 2006, the two vast oval rooms upstairs still show off the famous paintings to his specification. In the gallery space downstairs is the Jean Walter and Paul Guillaume Collection, an exceptional array of works by artists including Cézanne, Renoir, Matisse, Picasso, Soutine, Modigliani, Utrillo and Henri Rousseau.

PLACE DE LA CONCORDE

In 1753, Ange-Jacques Gabriel designed the vast **place de la Concorde** ❽ as place Louis XV, but the Revolutionaries later dispensed with all royal connotations. The King's statue was replaced with a guillotine, used to behead Louis XVI and over 1,000 other victims. In 1934, the square was the scene of bloody anti-government rioting by French fascists.

In the centre of the square is a pink-granite, 23m (75ft) tall Obelisk, a gift from

Death toll

According to official estimates, 1,119 people were decapitated on place de la Concorde, including Louis XVI, his queen Marie-Antoinette, Charlotte Corday, the poet André Chénier and, ironically, even the Revolutionary leader Robespierre.

Mohammed Ali, viceroy of Egypt. Dating from 1300 BC and once part of the temple of Ramses II in Luxor, it was erected here in 1836.

The two horses guarding the entrance to the Champs-Élysées are replicas of the 18th century *Horses of Marly*, sculpted by Guillaume Coustou (originals are in the Louvre).

THE GRANDS BOULEVARDS

North of the Louvre and Tuileries are the Grand Boulevards, a line of wide avenues running from west to east. The boulevards date from the 17th century, when Louis XIV tore down the medieval walls around Paris and created broad, tree-lined spaces. In the 19th century Baron Haussmann extended the string westwards, and the western end of what was named boulevard Haussmann became the preserve of the rich. High-street clothing chains now dominate stretches of the central boulevards, although traces of Second Empire extravagance can still be seen in the ornate balconies and facades.

PALAIS GARNIER

Dominating the place de l'Opéra is the city's historic opera house, the **Palais Garnier** ❾ (www.operadeparis.fr; daily 10am–5pm; guided tours in English Wed, Sat and Sun 11.30am and 2.30pm, daily July–Aug and school holidays; charge), where opera and ballet are performed in tandem with the newer Opéra Bastille (see page 54).

In 1860 architect Charles Garnier was commissioned by Napoleon III to build an opera house. His lavish designs were truly in tune with the pomp and opulence that characterised the Second Empire. A six-ton chandelier dominates the five-tiered auditorium, which is dripping with velvet and gilt. Marc Chagall painted the auditorium ceiling in 1964. Tours also take in the library and museum, showcasing scores, costumes and sets.

Overlooking the Grands Boulevards

MADELEINE

A stock exchange, the Bank of France, a theatre; these were among the uses proposed for the huge neoclassical church of **La Madeleine** ⑩ (daily 9.30am–7pm), on place de la Madeleine. Building first began in the 18th century, but stalled until Napoleon commissioned the current church in the 19th century as a temple to the glory of his army. Its colonnaded exterior with a heavily sculpted pediment, emulates a Roman temple such as the Maison Carrée in Nîmes. La Madeleine's political role was eventually muted when the Arc de Triomphe was built. The restored monarchy opted to use the Madeleine as a church, and the building was finally consecrated in 1842. Climb the steps for great views down rue Royale to place de la Concorde and the Assemblée Nationale.

Place de la Madeleine is home to luxury food shops, including Fauchon (nicknamed 'millionaire's supermarket'), luxury chocolatier Hédiard and truffle retailers Maison de la Truffe.

Also on the square is the **Kiosque-Théâtre Madeleine** (Tue–Sat 12.30–8pm, Sun until 4pm), where you can buy half-price seats for same-day theatre shows.

PLACE VENDÔME

Louis XIV wanted this square to be an imposing setting for a monument to him, but after it was laid out in 1699, only his financiers could afford the rent. Today the Ministry of Justice shares the square with banks, jewellers and the Ritz hotel. The statue of Louis XIV was overthrown during the Revolution. Its replace-ment, the Vendôme column,

The Vendôme column

commemorates the victories of Napoleon and is modelled on Trajan's Column in Rome. Cast from 1,250 Austrian cannons captured at Austerlitz, it is topped by a statue of the emperor. Like him, it was toppled, in the 1871 Commune (see page 21) at the instigation of the painter Gustave Courbet, who had to pay to have it re-erected two years later.

BEAUBOURG, LES HALLES & THE MARAIS

Sandwiched between the Louvre and Palais-Royal to the west and the Marais to the east, Beaubourg and Les Halles form one of the city's busiest commercial and cultural centres. The biggest landmark is the Centre Pompidou, Paris's modern art museum. For centuries, the Marais district was home to Paris' aristocrats. Today, it is an elegant, characterful district, with fine mansions, museums, attractive boutiques, kosher grocers, gay bars and hip cafés bundled together in a labyrinth of narrow streets.

CHÂTELET AND HÔTEL DE VILLE

Busy Place du Châtelet is a good starting point for exploring the area. Flanked by two theatres (Théâtre de la Ville and Théâtre du Châtelet), the square lies above one of Paris's biggest Métro and RER stations.

Opening out at the eastern end of avenue Victoria is the wide esplanade of the **Hôtel de Ville** ⑪ (Mon–Sat 10am–7pm; free), the ornate home of the city council. The neo-Renaissance building, with its magnificent Mansard roof, was rebuilt after the 17th century town hall was destroyed by fire in the 1871 Commune. In medieval times, place de l'Hôtel de Ville was the site of hangings and executions, but today, the pedestrianised square is considerably more alluring, especially in the evening when the fountains are floodlit. There is an ice-skating rink here in winter.

CENTRE POMPIDOU

'That'll get them screaming,' said then-President Georges Pompidou, as he approved the plans for the cultural centre bearing his name. The **Centre Pompidou** ⑫ (www.centre pompidou.fr; Wed–Mon 11am–10pm, Thu and for some exhibitions until 11pm; charge) was built by architects Richard Rogers, Renzo Piano and Gianfranco Franchini, and its inside-out design, dominated by external pipes, tubes, scaffolds and escalators, caused controversy when unveiled in 1977. The pipes are not just for show: the blue ones convey air, the green ones carry water, the yellow ones contain the electrics, and the red ones conduct heating.

The building, more popularly known as Beaubourg after its 13th-century neighbourhood, houses a cinema, library, design centre, music 'laboratory' and museum. The plaza outside is a popular rendezvous point and the site of the Stravinsky Fountain, featuring colourful sculptures by Niki de Saint Phalle.

One of the world's finest collections of 20th-century art, the **Musée National d'Art Moderne** (National Museum of Modern Art) is housed on the fourth and fifth floors, with the fifth floor home to modern works from 1905 to the 1960s, and the fourth floor covering contemporary work from the 1960s to the present day. Highlights of the modern period include works by Kandinsky, Klee, Klein, Matisse, Picasso and Pollock, and sections on Dadaism, Bauhaus and Surrealism. The contemporary collection includes pieces by Andy Warhol, Verner Panton, Joseph Beuys, Gerhard Richter and Jean Dubuffet. On

The inside-out Centre Pompidou

level six are temporary exhibitions and the fashionable, minimalist – and expensive – Georges restaurant (www.beaumarly.com).

Included in the price of the ticket to the Musée National d'Art Moderne is a visit to a reconstruction of sculptor Constantin Brancusi's studio, **Atelier Brancusi** (Wed–Mon 2–6pm).

The colourful Stravinsky Fountain

LES HALLES

For centuries this was the site of the capital's main food market, but to widespread regret, the 19th-century iron-and-glass pavilions were demolished in 1971. The market is now located out of town, near Orly. The much disliked partly-subterranean **Forum des Halles** shopping centre took their place, along with its gardens and playgrounds. These are in the process of being swept away as part of a colossal (and behind schedule) renovation programme that, it is hoped, will revitalise the area.

Near Les Halles is the Renaissance **Fontaine des Innocents**, once part of a cemetery. Bars and restaurants line the adjoining rue Berger and the streets leading off it. Some of the side streets have a seedy feel, and nearby rue St-Denis, once primarily a red-light district, still has a number of sex shops, and prostitutes at its northern end.

The church of **St-Eustache** (Mon–Fri 9.30am–7pm, Sat–Sun from 9am) dominates the north side of Les Halles. Built from 1532 to 1637, the main structure is late Gothic with an imposing Renaissance colonnade on its western facade. The church stages free organ recitals at 5.30pm on Sundays.

THE MARAIS

This district, to the north of the Île de la Cité and Île St-Louis, has successfully withstood the onslaught of modern construction. It provides a remarkably intact record of the development of the city, from the reign of Henri IV at the end of the 16th century to the advent of the Revolution. Built on reclaimed marshland, as its name suggests (*marais* means 'swamp'), the **Marais** contains some of Europe's most elegant Renaissance mansions (*hôtels*), many of which now serve as museums and libraries. In the 1960s, the government designated the area an historical monument, and conservation and restoration took hold. The big change in the last 25 years has been the steady influx of trendy boutiques and gay bars.

Take the métro to Rambuteau and start at the corner of rue des Archives and rue des Francs-Bourgeois, named after the

Fontaine des Innocents

poor (not bourgeois at all) who were allowed to live here tax-free in the 14th century. The national archives of the Ancien Régime are stored in an 18th-century mansion, the **Hôtel de Soubise** (Mon, Wed–Fri 10am–5.30pm, Sat–Sun 2–5.30pm; charge). Across a vast, horseshoe-shaped courtyard, you come across the rococo style of Louis XV's time in the apartments of the Prince and Princess of Soubise.

Eating al fresco in the historic Marais district

A short walk north of here, with its entrance on rue Réaumur, is the wonderful **Musée des Arts et Métiers** ⑬ (www.arts-et-metiers.net; Tue–Sun 10am–6pm, Thu until 9.30pm; charge) – nothing, in fact, to do with 'arts and trades', but instead Europe's oldest science museum. It has a vast collection of treasures ranging from ancient clocks and barometers to the first ever steam-powered vehicle, an enormous 1938 TV set and dozens of vintage cars, all housed in a former Benedictine priory.

A CLUSTER OF MUSEUMS

The Marais is home to a number of prestigious museums, including, on rue des Francs-Bourgeois, the grand **Musée Carnavalet** ⑭ (www.carnavalet.paris.fr; Tue–Sun 10am–6pm; free), which charts the history of the city. The museum is housed in the magnificent Hôtel Carnavalet, which was once home to the lady of letters Madame de Sévigné.

Nearby at 5 rue Thorigny, the truly excellent **Musée National Picasso** ⑮ (www.musee-picasso.fr; Tue-Sun: 9.30am – 6pm; until 9pm the 3rd Friday of the month) is set within the restored

Musée Carnavalet

Hôtel Salé. The museum's collections include more than 200 paintings, 158 sculptures and hundreds of drawings, engravings, ceramics and models for stage sets and costumes drawn from the artist's personal collection, as well as works by Braque, Matisse, Miró, Degas, Renoir and Rousseau.

Another Marais museum, housed in the Hôtel Donon at 8 rue Elzévir, is the **Musée Cognacq-Jay** (www.cognacq-jay.paris.fr; Tue–Sun 10am–6pm; free), which contains a splendid collection of 18th century paintings, furniture and *objets d'art*, bequeathed to the city by the founders of La Samaritaine. This grand old department store (at Châtelet), known for its impressive Art Deco interior, was closed in 2005, ostensibly for safety reasons. The current owner, luxury goods conglomerate LVMH, is converting it into a luxury hotel, Cheval Blanc, and boutiques.

There are a number of other hôtels of note in the district that are closed to the public, but can still be admired from the outside. These include the Hôtel d'Albret, Hôtel d'Aumont, Hôtel de Beauvais, Hôtel de Sens and Hôtel de Sully.

PLACE DES VOSGES

Rue des Francs-Bourgeois ends at what many agree is the most attractive residential square in Paris, **place des Vosges** (originally place Royale). Henri IV had it laid out in 1605 on the site of an old horse-market, the idea being to have 'all the houses in the same symmetry'. After the wedding festivities of his son Louis XIII, the gardens became the fashionable place in which to promenade, and later, a spot for aristocratic duels.

The Romantic writer Victor Hugo lived at No. 6, now a **museum** (Mon, Wed–Sat 10am–6pm, Sun 2–6pm; charge) housing a small collection of his artefacts. It is worth visiting to see the interior of one of the square's grand mansions.

JEWISH QUARTER

As the Marais has become popular with bar and boutique owners, the Jewish community has retreated to a small pocket centred on Rue des Rosiers, which is lined with kosher delis and falafel stands. Jewish history is told at the **Musée d'Art et d'Histoire du Judaïsme ⓰** (www.mahj.org; Mon–Fri 11am–6pm, Sun 10am–6pm; charge) on rue du Temple. The **synagogue**, with its Art Nouveau facade by Hector Guimard, is at 4 rue Pavée.

BASTILLE & EASTERN PARIS

For years a run-down area, Bastille was given a shot in the arm by the construction of a new opera house in the late 20th century. The area south of here, Bercy, has since become a potent symbol of urban regeneration, with a disused 19th-century railway viaduct and dilapidated wine warehouse district brought back to life and now thriving.

City bike scheme

Since its launch in 2007, the city council's Vélib' automated cycle hire scheme has steadily grown and improved. There are 1,800 stations across the capital, which means, on average, one every 300m (990ft). The bikes are rather heavy and utilitarian, but they are all in good working order, and prices are very reasonable; what's more, there is no charge for journeys under 30 minutes. For details, visit http://en.velib.paris.fr.

Enchanting Place des Vosges

BASTILLE

No trace of the prison stormed in 1789 remains on the **place de la Bastille**. Even the column in the centre commemorates a later revolution, that of 1830. The area was largely ignored, until the **Opéra Bastille** (www.operadeparis.fr), one of Mitterrand's *grands projets* (see page 23) was built. Cutting-edge artists and designers, like Jean-Paul Gaultier, moved into the area, and now, in streets such as rue de la Couronne, traditional shops alternate with galleries and cool restaurants. North of the Bastille are rue Oberkampf and rue Jean-Pierre Timbaud, where there is a concentration of hip bars and boutiques.

To the south of the Bastille are the quirky shops and cafés of Canal St-Martin, while at 15–121 avenue Daumesnil is the **Viaduc des Arts** (www.leviaducdesarts.com). In the golden age of rail, the Viaduc de Paris, built in 1859, supported a train line from Bastille to the Bois de Vincennes. However, as the railways declined in the 20th century, the viaduct fell into disrepair. It was saved from demolition and reopened in 1998, with attractive glass-fronted workshops and craft boutiques occupying its arches.

EASTERN PARIS

In **Bercy**, old stone-walled warehouses and cobbled streets have been given a new lease of life in the shape of Bercy Village, centred on cour St-Emilion, home to boutiques, restaurants and cafés. On the north side of the Parc de Bercy, a repurposed Frank Gehry building became the new home of the **Cinémathèque Française** (see page 96), housing a film museum, research centre, repertory cinema, restaurant and film archive. Pedestrians and cyclists can cross to the Left Bank on the city's newest bridge, the nearby Passerelle Simone de Beauvoir, which opened in 2006.

Also northeast of the Bastille is **Belleville**, home to an attractive park with panoramic views of Paris.

CHAMPS-ÉLYSÉES, TROCADÉRO & WEST

The **Champs-Élysées** ⓲ were designed by landscape architect André Le Nôtre in 1667 as an extension of the Tuileries (see page 41). Initially the promenade only reached as far as the Rond-Point des Champs-Élysées, less than half its current length. Over a hundred years passed before the rest of the avenue, stretching up to the Arc de Triomphe, was completed. Its reputation has ebbed and flowed with the centuries, and it is currently experiencing something of a comeback as one of the city's most prestigious shopping strips.

CHAMPS-ÉLYSÉES

The commercial stretch of the **Champs-Élysées** runs from the Rond-Point lo the Arc de Triomphe. The landmark stores are a four-storey, multi-brand shopping arcade, LE66, at No. 66; Guerlain at No. 68, with its Rococo-style facade and sumptuous interior; the Aladdin's cave of beauty products, Sephora, at No. 70; and Louis Vuitton at No. 101. There are cars as well as handbags: the glass-fronted Citroën showroom, at no. 42, displays current and historic models, and the freshly renovated Atelier Renault, at no. 53, has a swish mezzanine restaurant and cocktail bar.

The majority of designer shops are concentrated around avenue Montaigne, the southern end of avenue George V and rue du Faubourg St-Honoré. This is high fashion land, where prices for the majority are prohibitive.

On the southern side of the Champs, between place Clémenceau and the river, is the imposing, glass-domed **Grand Palais** ⑲ (www.grandpalais.fr; open during exhibitions only, times vary), constructed for the 1900 World Fair. The Grand Palais hosts several major art exhibitions every year; the colossal building also houses the **Palais de la Découverte**

PÈRE LACHAISE CEMETERY

The Cimetière du Père Lachaise (www.pere-lachaise.com; Mon–Fri 8am–6pm, Sat 8.30am–6pm, Sun 9am–6pm, closes at 5.15pm in winter) has seen an estimated 1,350,000 burials since its foundation in 1804. It even served as a battleground in 1871, when the Communards made a last stand here: the Mur des Fédérés in the southeast corner marks the place where many of them were executed by firing squad. Tombs of the famous include those of the painter Ingres, dancer Isadora Duncan, composers Rossini and Chopin, and writers such as Molière, Balzac, Proust and Oscar Wilde; the latter honoured with a fine monument by Jacob Epstein. Other famous names include singers Edith Piaf and Jim Morrison, and actress Marie Trintignant.

(www.palais-decouverte.fr; Tue–Sat 9.30am–6pm, Sun and bank hols 10am–7pm; charge), which includes a hands-on exhibition of the sciences, with a planetarium as centrepiece.

Across avenue Winston Churchill is the **Petit Palais**, which houses the fine-art collection of the Musée des Beaux-Arts de la Ville de Paris (www.petitpalais.paris.fr; Tue–Sun 10am–6pm, temporary exhibitions until 8pm Thu; free but charge for temporary exhibitions).

The Champs-Élysées seen from the top of the Arc de Triomphe

ARC DE TRIOMPHE

The circular area at the top of the Champs-Élysées is popularly known to Parisians as *l'Etoile* (the star), after the 12 avenues branching out from its centre. Officially renamed **place Charles de Gaulle** after the death of the president in 1970, it is dominated by one of the most familiar Paris icons, the **Arc de Triomphe** ⑳ (www.monuments-nationaux.fr; daily 10am–10.30pm, Apr–Sept until 11pm; charge). The arch is 50m (164ft) high and 45m (148ft) wide. A trip to the top of the staircase (lift for the disabled only) affords excellent views. It is from here that you can best appreciate the *tour de force* of geometric planning that the avenues represent.

Napoleon I conceived of the Arc de Triomphe as a trib-ute to his armies, and it bears the names of hundreds of

Famous macaroons

Renowned in Paris for generations for its delectable macaroons, Ladurée (www.laduree.fr), a bakery/restaurant at 75 avenue des Champs-Élysées, is always busy and very chic. Don't leave without trying the melt-in-the-mouth macaroons, which come in a multitude of flavours. There are other branches in the city.

his marshals and generals, and dozens of victories. No defeats are recorded, naturally, although a few of the victories are debatable. Napoleon himself only ever saw a wood-and-canvas model, since the arch was not completed until the 1830s. It rapidly became the focus for state occasions, such as the return of the emperor's remains from St Helena in 1840 and the funeral of Victor Hugo in 1885. At the Liberation, this was the spot where General de Gaulle began his triumphal march down the Champs-Élysées.

Under the arch is the grave of the Unknown Soldier. Since 1920, it has been the last resting place of a soldier who died in World War I. The eternal flame was lit here in 1923.

TROCADÉRO

Dominating place du Trocadéro is the **Palais de Chaillot** ㉑, built for the Paris World Fair of 1937. The imposing Art Deco palace was designed in the shape of an amphitheatre, with its wings following the original outline of the old Trocadéro in graceful symmetry. The west wing is home to the **Musée de la Marine** (www.musee-marine.fr; Wed–Mon 11am–6pm, Sat–Sun until 7pm; charge), which traces the history of the French navy. Also here is the recently renovated Musée de l'Homme (www.museedelhomme.fr) also known as the 'Museum of Mankind'. The east wing houses the **Cité de l'Architecture et du Patrimoine** (www.citechaillot.fr; Wed–Mon 11am–7pm, Thu until 9pm; charge), opened in 2007, which combines

Paris's old architecture museum with the Institut Français d'Architecture.

On avenue des Nations-Unies is **Cinéaqua** (www.cineaqua. com; daily 10am–7pm; charge), a vast aquarium with cinema and animation studio. There are dozens of tanks containing some 9,000 fish, grouped in mini marine ecosystems.

Down avenue du Président Wilson is the vast **Palais de Tokyo ㉒**, built as the Electricity Pavilion for the 1937 World Fair. One wing was intended to hold post-1905 fine art from the municipal fine-art collection; the other wing (now the Site de Création Contemporaine) was planned for the national collection of modern art.

The **Musée d'Art Moderne de la Ville de Paris** (www. mam.paris.fr; Tue–Sun 10am–6pm, Thu until 10pm during exhibitions; free but charge for temporary exhibitions) opened there in 1961. In 1977 the core collection of French and international art was given a new home at the Centre Pompidou. Whereas the emphasis at the Centre Pompidou is on international art, here the focus is on artists who worked in Paris.

In the other wing is the **Site de Création Contemporaine** (www.palaisdetokyo.com; Wed–Mon noon–midnight; charge), where a multidisciplinary programme

Arc de Triomphe

focuses on young artists through exhibitions, performances and workshops.

Opposite the Palais de Tokyo to the north is the newly reopened Musée Galliéra/Musée de la Mode de la Ville de Paris (10 avenue Pierre 1er de Serbie; www.galliera.paris.fr), which houses the city's collection of clothes and accessories dating from the 18th century to the present day.

WESTERN PARIS

West of the Palais de Chaillot, Passy is an upmarket, villagey residential area with a couple of busy shopping streets (rue de Passy and rue de l'Assomption). It is also home to the atmospheric **Maison de Balzac** (47 rue Raynouard; www.balzac.paris.fr; Tue–Sun 10am–6pm; free), where the writer penned much of his great opus *La Comédie Humaine*. The house remains furnished as it would have been at the time, with a rich collection of Balzacian manuscripts and memorabilia on show.

Also in the west of Paris is the **Musée Marmottan-Monet** (2 rue Louis-Boilly; www.marmottan.com; Tue–Sun 10am–6pm, Thu until 8pm; charge), showcase for the art assembled by

APP HAPPY

With the near ubiquity of smart phones and tablet computers, it is no surprise that Paris is producing some very handy applications for use on the go. One of the best is the RATP public transport authority's slick, free guide to its entire network, with live traffic updates, maps and route planning capabilities. Another free guide is produced by the Louvre, and has maps of the museum and useful background on its most popular exhibits. If you're in Paris during August, install the city council's Paris-Plages app, which tells you all you need to know about the annual riverside 'beach' and associated events.

The Musée d'Art Moderne de la Ville de Paris

collector Louis Marmottan (1856–1932). The displays are comprised mostly of Impressionist masterpieces, including works by Monet, Renoir, Manet and Gauguin, but there is also some exceptional First Empire furniture.

BOIS DE BOULOGNE

In western Paris is the capital's biggest park, comprising 900 hectares (2,200 acres) of grassland, lakes and woods. Inspired by Hyde Park in London, Napoleon III commissioned Baron Haussmann to transform a remnant of an old hunting forest into a public park. The plans included the **Bagatelle**, once a royal retreat, which now has both manicured and English-landscape style gardens. Also within the park is a craft museum, a boating lake, the **Jardin d'Acclimatation** (www.jardindacclimatation.fr) amusement park with attractions for children, and two racecourses: Longchamp for flat races; Auteuil for steeplechases. However, parts of the park after dark are considered to be among the most dangerous places in Paris.

AROUND MONCEAU

Overlooking Parc Monceau, the **Musée Nissim de Camondo** (63 rue de Monceau; www.lesartsdecoratifs.fr; Wed–Sun 10am–5.30pm; charge) was built by a wealthy Jewish banking family in the style of the Petit Trianon (see page 87) at Versailles. The remarkable collection of tapestries, carpets, porcelain, furniture and paintings, all dating from the 18th century, were bequeathed to the state in 1935 by the passionate art collector, Count Moïse de Camondo, in memory of his son, Nissim, killed in action in 1917. The building and family history are as fascinating as the collection.

Sacré-Cœur

Also beside Parc Monceau is the **Musée Cernuschi** (7 avenue Vélasquez; www.cernuschi.paris.fr; Tue–Sun 10am–6pm; free), one of the most important collections of Oriental art in Europe. The 19th-century financier Henri Cernuschi amassed the collection on a tour of China and Japan, and built this mansion to house it.

South of Parc Monceau, at 158 boulevard Haussmann, is the **Musée Jacquemart-André 23** (www.musee-jacquemart-andre.com; daily 10am–6pm, until 8.30pm Mon and Sat during exhibitions; charge). The museum displays art and furniture that once belonged to wealthy collector Edouard André and his wife, erstwhile society portrait painter Nélie Jacquemart. The house is magnificent, and its fine-art collection includes works by Bellini, Boucher, David, Donatello, Uccello, Rembrandt and Titian. The gorgeous café, decorated with chandeliers and antiques, is also worth a visit.

MONTMARTRE & PIGALLE

With narrow, winding streets and dead-ends, **Montmartre** ('*la Butte*', or the hill, to its residents) still has something of a provincial feel. For over 200 years it has been associated with artists and bohemians. The tourist *Montmartrobus* (www.ratp. fr) spares you the walk and shows you some of the area in a single sweep, but the best way to discover Montmartre at your own pace is to start early, at the top. Take the Métro to Abbesses and the lift to the street (the stairs here seem endless) – and note the handsome Art Nouveau entrance as you leave. Rue Yvonne le Tac leads to the base station of a funicular railway.

SACRÉ-CŒUR

The funicular (Métro/bus tickets are valid) climbs to the terrace right in front of the Byzantine-style basilica of **Sacré-Cœur** ㉔ (www.sacre-coeur-montmartre.com; basilica daily 6am–10.30pm, crypt and dome 9am–6pm, until 7pm in summer; charge for crypt and dome). Standing at the highest point in Paris, it is one of the city's principal landmarks, even if some people still scorn it as a vulgar pastiche. The Sacré-Cœur's white appearance comes from the local Château-Landon limestone, which bleaches on contact with carbon dioxide in the air and hardens with age. For many, the best reason to visit the basilica is the view of the city from the dome or the terrace below.

Moulin Rouge – you can't miss it

PLACE DU TERTRE

A few steps west of Sacré-Cœur is **St-Pierre-de-Montmartre**, one of the city's oldest churches. Consecrated in 1147, it is a significant work of the early Gothic style, belied by its 18th century facade. Nearby **place du Tertre** was once the centre of village life. The square is best visited early in the morning, before the pushy portrait artists set up their easels and the crowds of tourists take over.

On place Emile Goudeau, just downhill but artistically on an altogether much higher level, No. 13 was the site of the studio known as the **Bateau-Lavoir** (so-called because the building resembled the Seine's laundry boats until it was destroyed by fire). It was here that Picasso, Georges Braque and Juan Gris developed Cubism, Modigliani painted, and Apollinaire wrote his first Surrealist verses. Some of their predecessors – Renoir, Van Gogh and Gauguin – once lived and worked just north of place du Tertre.

The **Cimetière de Montmartre** ㉕ (daily 8am–6pm, Sat 8.30am–6pm, Sun 9am–6pm) is at 20 avenue Rachel. The cemetery's more illustrious tenants include composers Berlioz and Offenbach, the sculptor Degas, German poet Heinrich Heine and film director François Truffaut.

PIGALLE

At the far end of rue Lepic, a market street renowned for its food shops and several appealingly bohemian cafés, is place Blanche, where the ambience changes. On the corner of boulevard de Clichy is the iconic **Moulin Rouge** (see page 97), still staging its nightly cabarets, although mostly to tourists. Next door is **La Machine**, a huge disco, pumping with the sounds of house, dance music and mainstream pop. Less artistic attractions abound in **Pigalle**, a powerhouse of the Paris sex trade for decades. Tassled curtains provide glimpses of smoky interiors, garish signs promote live sex shows and pushy bouncers attempt to entice passers-by.

However, Pigalle's sleaze has been tempered by trendy nightlife venues. The cabarets that formerly occupied half the houses along rue des Martyrs are increasingly being taken over by hip clubs and fashionable bars.

LA VILLETTE

In northeast Paris, right against the Périphérique ring road, is the **Parc de la Villette** ㉖ (Métro: Porte de Pantin or Porte de la Villette, www.villette.com). Laid out on the site of an enormous abattoir, which was rendered obsolete by improved refrigeration techniques and poor design (the cows could not get up the steps), 55 hectares (136 acres) of futuristic gardens surround a colossal science museum, the **Cité des Sciences et de l'Industrie** (www.cite-sciences.fr; Tue–Sat 10am–6pm, Sun until 7pm; charge).

La Géode

Begin at 'L'Univers' (Universe), which has a spectacular planetarium and also provides an explanation of the Big Bang. 'La Vie' (Life) is an eclectic mix of medicine, agriculture and economics. 'La Matière' (Matter) reproduces a nuclear explosion and gives you the chance to land an Airbus 320, and 'La Communication' has displays of artificial intelligence, three-dimensional graphics and virtual reality. On the ground floor is the Cité des Enfants, which has interactive exhibits and activities for children aged 2–12 years. Outside the main entrance is L'Argonaute, a retired naval submarine.

La Géode (www.lageode.fr; Mon times vary, Tue–Thu 10.30am–6.30pm, Fri–Sun until 8.30pm; charge) is a giant silver ball housing a wraparound imax cinema.

The former cattle market now houses a cultural and conference centre in the immense 19th century Grande Halle. Next door, the **Cité de la Musique** is an edifice of angles designed by architect Christian de Portzamparc, and includes the **Musée de la Musique** (www.cite-musique.fr; Tue–Sat noon–6pm, Sun 10am–6pm; charge). Portzamparc also designed the national music and dance conservatory on the other side of the Grande Halle. The museum charts the development of classical, jazz and folk music and houses an impressive collection of over 4,500 musical instruments.

The impressive gardens of the park are the biggest to be built in Paris since Haussmann's time. Designed by Bernard Tschumi and opened in 1993, they comprise several thematic areas such as the Jardin des Frayeurs Enfantines (Garden of Childhood Fears) with a huge dragon slide, and the Jardin des Vents (Garden of Winds), home to multicoloured bamboo. Abstraction continues in the form of Tschumi's folies: red angular 'tree houses' (minus the trees), each with a special function such as play area, workshop, daycare centre or café.

LATIN QUARTER & ST-GERMAIN-DES-PRÉS

The area referred to as the Latin Quarter lies to the east of boulevard St-Michel. This maze of ancient streets and squares has been the stamping ground of students for nearly eight centuries and it is home to the city's most famous university, the Sorbonne. Latin was virtually the mother tongue until Napoleon put a stop to it after the Revolution. West of boulevard St-Michel is St-Germain-des-Prés, once the centre of literary Paris and existentialism, with the oldest church in Paris at its heart. Although these two areas have changed over the past few decades, with high fashion increasingly replacing heavy thinking, they still maintain their charm in tree-lined boulevards, narrow streets and beautifully manicured gardens.

ALONG THE CANAL

The Paris canals were dug in 1821 as a transport link for the factories and warehouses in the area northeast of the Bastille. Shielded by trees, the canal is a popular strolling ground, particularly on balmy summer evenings. A pleasant way to experience it is by canal boat, starting either at Bastille or at La Villette. Canal tours lasting around two and a half hours are run by Canauxrama (tel: 01 42 39 15 00; www.canauxrama.com).

THE LATIN QUARTER

Begin your visit to the Latin Quarter at **place St-Michel**, where students buy their books or gather around the grand 1860s fountain by Gabriel Davioud. From here, plunge into the narrow streets of the **St-Séverin** quarter to the east (rues St-Séverin, de la Harpe and Galande). Here, you will find medieval streets teeming with Greek restaurants, Tunisian bakeries selling sticky date pastries, and art-house cinemas.

The early Gothic church of **St-Julien-le-Pauvre**, located on the street of the same name, hosts regular recitals of chamber and religious music. Just across rue St-Jacques stands the exquisite 13th to 15th century flamboyant Gothic church of **St-Séverin**, in which Dante is said to have prayed and French composer Camille Saint-Saëns asked to be made honorary organist.

St-Germain-des-Prés still trades on its literary heyday

THE SORBONNE

Named after the 13th-century college established by Robert de Sorbon for poor theological students, the university was later taken in hand by Cardinal Richelieu, who financed its reconstruction (1624–42). Few of the somewhat forbidding buildings are open to the public, but you can go inside the 17th century **courtyard** with its ornate sundial and see the outside of the Baroque library and domed church.

Second-hand book stall

Protests against overcrowding, antiquated teaching, bureaucracy and the basis of the social system made the Sorbonne a focal point for unrest in 1968, a year of ferment across Europe. Over on the tree-shaded **place de la Sorbonne**, it is hard to imagine the police invading such a peaceful sanctuary, one that for centuries guaranteed student immunity. But invade they did, and revolt exploded onto the streets. Students and workers made common cause, and there followed widespread national strikes that threatened the survival of the government. In the aftermath of the revolts, the Sorbonne was absorbed into the huge Paris Universities monolith and lost its independence.

MUSÉE NATIONAL DU MOYEN AGE – THERMES DE CLUNY

Opposite the Sorbonne's rue des Ecoles entrance is the **Musée National du Moyen Age** ❷❼ (6 place Paul-Painlevé; www. musee-moyenage.fr; Wed–Mon 9.15am–5.45pm; charge), still often called by its former name, the Musée de Cluny. Once the

Musée National du Moyen Age

residence of the Abbots of Cluny, the museum houses one of the world's finest collections of medieval artefacts. Its star attraction is the exquisite, 15th-century tapestry *La Dame à la Licorne* (The Lady and the Unicorn), six pieces depicting the five senses and the temptations that the eponymous lady vows to overcome. The museum also holds 21 of the original heads of the Kings of Judah, sculpted in 1220 for Notre-Dame cathedral, but vandalised in the Revolution.

The Hôtel de Cluny was built on the remains of a huge Gallo-Roman bath house believed to have been erected in ad200 by the guild of *nautes* (boatmen); ships' prows are carved on the arch supports of the frigidarium (cold bath house).

PANTHÉON

Designed in 1755 as the church of Ste-Geneviève (patron saint of Paris), the neoclassical **Panthéon** ㉘ (www.monuments-nationaux.fr; daily Oct–Mar 10am–6pm, Apr– Sept until 6.30pm; charge) was requisitioned during the Revolution to serve as a mausoleum. In the 19th century its status oscillated between secular and sacred, but Victor Hugo's funeral in 1885 settled the issue in favour of a secular mausoleum. The interior is sparse, its walls covered with 19th century murals by Puvis de Chavannes. The crypt is a maze of corridors lined with cells containing tombs.

RUE MOUFFETARD

The old streets behind the Panthéon, where the bustling **rue Mouffetard** and its offshoots meet, are like a small town within the city. The stalls of rue Mouffetard's morning market are piled with appetising produce. Here, and on tiny **place de la Contrescarpe** nearby, you will find restaurants serving a wide range of international cuisine. A little to the east, signs to **Arènes de Lutèce** point to a little park that is the site of a Roman amphitheatre, partially restored after its remains were found in the 19th century.

In rue St-Etienne-du-Mont is the church of **St-Etienne-du-Mont** (Tue–Fri 8.45am–7.45pm, Sat–Sun 8.45am–noon, 2–7.45pm, school holidays Tue–Sun 10am–noon and 4–7.45pm). This was the parish church of the Abbey of Ste-Geneviève and still houses a shrine to the city's patron saint. The highlight is the Renaissance rood screen (1541), the only one in Paris.

INSTITUT DU MONDE ARABE

Back by the Seine, but heading east, stroll past the university complex that stands on the site of the former Halles aux Vins (wine market). Designed by architect Jean Nouvel, the nearby **Institut du Monde Arabe** ㉙ (1 rue des Fossés-St-Bernard; www.imarabe.org; Tue–Thu 10am–6pm, Fri until 9.30pm, Sat–Sun until 7pm; charge) was built with the help of 16 Arab nations to foster cultural links between Europe and the Islamic world. Inside,

Great thinkers

Among those interred in the Panthéon are novelist Emile Zola, socialist Jean Jaurès, Louis Braille and Pierre and Marie Curie.

a museum traces the cultures of the Arab world with first-rate exhibits. A library of over 40,000 volumes covers all aspects of Arab culture. There are fine views from the rooftop restaurant.

JARDIN DES PLANTES

Adjacent is the **Jardin des Plantes** (www.jardindesplantes.net; daily 8am–5.30pm, 7.30am–8pm in summer), created by Louis XIII as 'a royal garden of medicinal plants' and still a fine botanical and decorative garden, with exotic plants in the hothouses. The oldest tree in Paris is located here.

Institut du Monde Arabe

The adjoining **Muséum National d'Histoire Naturelle** (www.mnhn.fr; Wed–Mon 10am–6pm; charge) has renovated its venerable exhibits of fossils, skeletons, butterflies and mineral samples. The **Grande Galerie de l'Evolution** (36 rue Geoffroy-St-Hilaire; opening times as above), devoted to the origins of life on earth, is outstanding.

ST-GERMAIN-DES-PRÉS

Once the heart of literary Paris, **St-Germain-des-Prés** covers an area stretching roughly from St-Sulpice to the Seine and bounded to the west by boulevard St-Germain. Its elegant streets house chic boutiques, yet it still retains a sense of animation, with crowded cafés spilling out onto the pavements. In the 1950s the area became a breeding ground for literature and philosophy. Writers such as Jean-Paul Sartre, Simone de Beauvoir and Albert Camus, gathered at **Les Deux Magots**, **Café de Flore** and other venues.

Les Deux Magots

That said, the days of black polo-necks and beret-clad existentialists engaged in heated debate are over. The area has been colonised by designers and upmarket antiques dealers. The Marché St-Germain shows just how much it has changed. After a tasteful restoration, the old market hall now contains boutiques, a swimming pool, an auditorium and a food market.

On the opposite side of the boulevard, the church of **St-Germain-des-Prés** ❸⓪ (Mon–Sat 8am–7.45pm, Sun 9am–8pm) is the oldest in Paris, parts of it dating from the 11th century.

ACADÉMIE FRANÇAISE

The august Palais de l'Institut de France, home of the **Académie Française**, is north of the church of St-Germain, on quai de Conti by the Pont des Arts. It was designed by Louis le Vau in 1668 to harmonise with the Louvre across the river. The Institut began as a school for the sons of provincial gentry, financed by a legacy from Cardinal Mazarin. Then, in 1805, the building was turned over to the Institut, which comprises the Académie Française, supreme arbiter of the French language founded by Cardinal

Richelieu in 1635, and the Académies des Belles-Lettres, Sciences, Beaux-Arts, and Sciences Morales et Politiques.

MUSÉE DELACROIX AND ST-SULPICE

Tucked away in a tiny square a short walk from the church of St-Germain-des-Prés is the delightful **Musée National Eugène Delacroix** ㉛ (6 place Furstenberg; www.musee-delacroix.fr; Wed–Mon 9.30am–5pm; charge). The painter lived here from 1857 to 1863 while he was working on frescoes in a chapel at St-Sulpice. Temporary exhibitions are held in the airy former studio, and letters and personal effects are displayed in the house. There is a wonderfully calm garden out the back.

A short hop south across boulevard St-Germain-des-Prés is place St-Sulpice, the eastern side of which is dominated by Jean-Baptiste Servandoni's Italianesque church of the same name. **St-Sulpice** (daily 7.30am–7.30pm) is notable for its vast

NEW LEFT BANK

The 'new' Rive Gauche is the biggest urban renewal project since the mid-1850s. Newly created streets and buildings are going up in a zone of rusty factories and disused railway tracks that extend south along the river from the Gare d'Austerlitz. The area's centre-piece is the **Bibliothèque Nationale de France François Mitterrand** (www.bnf.fr; Mon 2–7pm, Tue–Sat 9am–7pm, Sun 1–7pm), opened in 1996; its 90m (300ft) high glass towers evoke open books. The newest high-profile addition to the area (opened 2012) is **Les Docks – Cité de la Mode et du Design** at 28 quai d'Austerlitz. Its bright green riverfront facade has been fixed on a disused warehouse that is home to the French fashion institute (www.ifm-paris.com). Hip shops, bars, clubs and restaurants are also here.

towers (under restoration), one of which is higher than the other, and for Delacroix's massive oil-and-wax frescoes, completed only two years before his death.

The Jardin du Luxembourg

JARDIN DU LUXEMBOURG

The beautifully landscaped **Jardin du Luxembourg** ㉜ is the quintessential Paris park. Students read, relax or play tennis, old men meet under the chestnut trees to play chess or a game of *boules*, lovers huddle together on metal chairs, and children sail boats across the carp-filled pond and ride a merry-go-round designed by Charles Garnier, architect of the historic opera house (see page 44). At the northern end of the gardens, the Italianate **Palais du Luxembourg** (guided tours one Saturday each month; tel: 01 44 54 19 30; www.senat. fr), built for Marie de Médicis in the early 17th century, now houses the French Senate. The adjacent Petit Luxembourg is the official home of the president of the Senate.

The **Musée du Luxembourg** (19 rue de Vaugirard; www. museeduluxembourg.fr; daily 10am–7.30pm, Mon and Fri until 10pm; charge) hosts art exhibitions.

ODÉON

The Odéon district lies between the Latin Quarter and St-Germain-des-Prés. Across boulevard St-Germain, at the Carrefour de l'Odéon, a statue of the Revolutionary leader Georges Danton marks the spot where his house once stood. Fellow Revolutionary Camille Desmoulins lived at No. 2 before storming the Bastille in 1789. Others plotted to the north in neighbouring streets that now shelter some of the most expensive boutiques and apartments in Paris.

From here, rue de l'Odéon, the first street in Paris to have gutters and pavements, leads to place de l'Odéon. The neo-classical **Odéon Théâtre de l'Europe** (tel: 01 44 85 40 40; www.theatre-odeon.eu), founded in 1782, is home to one of France's leading state theatre companies. It puts on a repertoire of mainly foreign playwrights (Büchner, Chekhov, Shakespeare, etc), sometimes in original-language productions.

AROUND THE EIFFEL TOWER

When the Paris nobility moved out of the Marais in the 18th century, and Versailles dwindled, the rich and famous built new town houses across the river from the Tuileries, in the 7th *arrondissement*. Not only is this chic district rich with upmarket architecture, it also has a wealth of visitor attractions, with highlights including the Musée d'Orsay, the Eiffel Tower, the Invalides and the Musée Rodin.

MUSÉE D'ORSAY

'The station is superb and truly looks like a Fine Arts Museum, and since the Fine Arts Museum resembles a station, I suggest... we make the change while we still can,' said painter Edouard Detaille in 1900. In 1986, his joke became a reality. Linked to the Tuileries by the Passerelle Léopold–Sédar-Senghor footbridge, the converted 19th-century hotel-cum-railway station was transformed into the **Musée d'Orsay** ③ (www.musee-orsay.fr; Tue–Sun 9.30am–6pm, Thu until 9.45pm; charge), devoted to French art from 1848 to 1914. Keeping the exterior much as it was, Italian architect Gae Aulenti adapted the interior to house many of the previously scattered works of that period, including the superb Impressionist collection formerly held in the Jeu de Paume (see page 42). Sculpture is well represented, and photography is covered from its inception (1839) onwards.

Many visitors start at the top with the Impressionists who include: Renoir, Cézanne, Manet and Monet before heading down to the mezzanine for the Post Impressionists, notably Van Gogh and Gauguin. Among the ground-floor collections, the vast canvases of Gustave Courbet are outstanding. There is a contemporary café high up behind the huge old station clock, and on the middle level is the station hotel's beautifully restored restaurant.

ASSEMBLÉE NATIONALE

Geographically if not temperamentally part of the Left Bank, the Palais Bourbon is the seat of the **Assemblée Nationale** (33 bis quai d'Orsay), the Lower House of the French Parliament. Built from 1722 to 1728 for Louis XIV's daughter the Duchess

Orsay's vast central sculpture aisle

of Bourbon, it forms a fittingly stately riverside facade for the grand 7th *arrondissement*. Built in the style of the Grand Trianon at Versailles, Napoleon later added the Grecian columns facing the Pont de la Concorde. The palace is more graceful when seen from its entrance on the south side. Only French citizens can go in, apart from on the annual Journées du Patrimoine open days, when thousands queue to see the Delacroix paintings in the library.

MUSÉE RODIN

The Prime Minister's residence, Hôtel Matignon (57 rue de Varenne), is a short walk from the Assemblée Nationale. Its private park has a music pavilion favoured for secret strategy sessions. On the same elegant street, at No. 77, Rodin's former mansion, the delightful 18th-century Hôtel Biron, is now a showcase for the sculptor's works in the form of the **Musée Rodin** ③④ (www.musee-rodin.fr; Tue–Sun 10am–5.45pm; charge). Many of the most famous sculptures are in the gardens (Oct–Mar closure at 5pm). Highlights include *The Kiss* (removed from the Chicago World Fair of 1893 for being too shocking), *The Thinker* (reputedly Dante contemplating the Inferno), *The Burghers of Calais* and *Balzac*, depicting the writer as a mountain of a man. Also on display are works by Camille Claudel, the most famous of Rodin's mistresses.

LES INVALIDES

One of the most important sights in this area is the monumental **Hôtel des Invalides** ③⑤ (www.invalides.org; daily 10am–5pm, Apr–Oct until 6pm; charge), established by Louis XIV as the first national hospital and retirement home for soldiers wounded in action. At one time it housed some 6,000 veterans, but Napoleon Bonaparte commandeered a large part of the building for the superb **Musée de l'Armée** (opening times as above), a vast collection of weapons and military paraphernalia dating from medieval times to the modern era. It is, in effect, several museums in one: there are large sections devoted to the two world wars, another to dozens of wonderfully intricate 18th century models of French towns and fortresses, another to awe-inspiring suits of armour, and a new section to uniforms in 2009.

The Invalides came to symbolise the glory of Napoleon himself, when his remains were brought back from St Helena in 1840 for burial in the chapel under the golden **Dôme** (opening times as above, July–Aug until 7pm). The emperor's son, who died of tuberculosis in Vienna, is buried in the crypt; his remains were sent here by Hitler in 1940.

The main courtyard allows access to the adjoining church of **St-Louis-des-Invalides**, decorated with flags taken by French armies in battle. The courtyard itself contains the 18 cannons, including eight taken from Vienna, that Napoleon ordered to be fired on great occasions, including the birth of his son in 1811. The cannons sounded again for the 1918 Armistice and the funeral of Marshal Foch in 1929.

Southwest of the Invalides is the **Ecole Militaire**, where officers have trained since

Rodin's The Thinker

Napoleon's tomb inside the Église du Dôme

the middle of the 18th century. Their former parade ground, the vast **Champ de Mars**, is now a green park stretching all the way to the Eiffel Tower.

THE EIFFEL TOWER

For many, the ultimate Paris monument is still the **Tour Eiffel** ㊱, or Eiffel Tower (www.tour-eiffel.fr; daily mid-June–Aug 9am–12.45am, last lift midnight, or 11pm for top floor, steps 9am–12.45am, Sept–mid-June 9.30am–11.45pm, last lift 11pm, or 10.30pm for top floor, steps 9.30am–6.30pm; charge). When Gustave Eiffel's icon was chosen as the centrepiece of the World Fair of 1889, he claimed enthusiastically, 'France will be the only country with a 300m flagpole!' But his designs were met with strong opposition. The architect of the opera house, Charles Garnier, and the novelist Guy de Maupassant were its most vocal opponents; Maupassant organised a protest picnic underneath it – 'the only place out of sight of the wretched construction'.

However, the Paris public loved their new tower, and only a few years later writers and artists such as Apollinaire, Jean Cocteau, Raoul Dufy and Maurice Utrillo heaped praise upon it. At 321m (1,054ft) the tower was the world's tallest building until 1931, when New York's Empire State Building went up. Surviving a proposal for its demolition in 1909, when the placing of a radio transmitter at the top gave it a valuable practical function, the tower is climbed by some 7 million visitors a year.

There are 360 steps to the first level, where there is an audio-visual presentation on the tower's history, and another 700 to the second, which now has an area with a glass floor; both of these floors are also accessible by lifts – there is always a queue for these, which travel 100,000km (62,137 miles) a year. On the third level (accessible by lift only) is a glassed-in viewing platform, a champagne bar and Gustave Eiffel's sitting room. On a clear day panoramas of over 65km (40 miles) can be enjoyed. There are two restaurants, including the Michelin-starred Jules Verne (see page 115) on the second floor. On hot days the ironwork expands, enabling the tower to grow as much as 15cm (6in). Even in the strongest of winds, it has never swayed more than 12cm (4in). Up to 40 tonnes of paint have to be used when it is painted every seven years.

The iconic Eiffel Tower

MUSÉE DU QUAI BRANLY

Just northeast of the tower, at 37 quai Branly, is Jacques Chirac's cultural legacy, the **Musée du Quai Branly** ❸ (www.quaibranly. fr; Tue, Wed and Sun 11am–7pm, Thu–Sat until 9pm; charge), opened in 2006. The museum houses a collection of around 300,000 objects of art from Africa, Asia, the Americas and Oceania, with over 3,600 items actually on display. With its colonial overtones, the collection has sparked some controversy, but the building itself – a striking foliage-covered scarlet edifice designed by Jean Nouvel – has been more warmly received.

MONTPARNASSE

Named after the mountain home of the classical Muses, 'Mount Parnassus' was a mound left after quarrying. In the 1920s, the quarter took over from Montmartre as the stamping ground of the city's artistic colony, led by Picasso. American expatriates such as Ernest Hemingway, Gertrude Stein, F. Scott Fitzgerald and John Dos Passos liked the free-living atmosphere and added to the mystique themselves.

One of Henry Miller's hangouts, Le Select (99 boulevard du Montparnasse) opened as an all-night bar in 1925. *Les Six*, the group of composers that included Milhaud, Poulenc and Honegger, met here. La Coupole (see page 115), just opposite at No. 102, was a favourite with literary couple Sartre and de Beauvoir in the years following World War II; it has been rebuilt and now seats 400 people. Le Dôme at No. 108 has lost some of its character since the days of Modigliani and Stravinsky, with elaborate remodelling. Across the street, at No. 105, Picasso, Derain and Vlaminck used to meet at La Rotonde. At the junction of boulevard du Montparnasse and boulevard St-Michel, La Closerie des Lilas is where Lenin and Trotsky dreamt of a Russian Revolution, and where Hemingway and his friends met after World War I.

Today the attraction isn't immediately evident: boulevard du Montparnasse is plain by Paris standards, and most of the haunts where the 'Lost Generation' found itself have been polished and painted, or even entirely rebuilt. But people still pay elevated prices for the privilege of sitting in a seat that may have been warmed by Modigliani, Lenin or Sartre.

The 59-storey, 210m (689ft) **Tour Montparnasse** (33 avenue du Maine; www.tourmontparnasse56.com; Apr–Sept daily 9.30am–11.30pm, Oct–Mar Sun–Thu until 10.30pm, Fri–Sat until 11pm, last lift half an hour before closing,) may be something of an egregious eyesore, but the view from the top is marvellous. Gourmets should visit Le Ciel de Paris, which claims to be the highest restaurant in Europe (above ground level).

The **Cimetière du Montparnasse** ③⑧ (entrance on boulevard Edgar Quinet, Mar–Nov 8am–6pm, Sat from 8.30am, Sun

A colourful mural in Montparnasse

The catacombs

Beneath Montparnasse are the city's catacombs (entrance on place Denfert-Rochereau; www.cata combes.paris.fr; Tue–Sun 10am–5pm; charge), old quarries whose corridors were used for the reburial of millions of skeletons from overcrowded cemeteries and charnel houses. Unidentified, the bones are stacked on shelves or artfully arranged into macabre patterns.

from 9am, slightly shorter hours in winter) contains the tombs of composers Saint-Saëns and César Franck, writer Maupassant and poet Baudelaire, plus Alfred Dreyfus, the Jewish army officer whose conviction on trumped-up spying charges split the nation. Also buried here are car-maker André Citroën, Vichy prime minister Pierre Laval (executed while dying from a suicide attempt) and philosopher Jean-Paul Sartre and his writer companion Simone de Beauvoir.

LA DÉFENSE

Follow the long avenue de la Grande-Armée down from the Arc de Triomphe, and the battery of towers looms larger and larger beyond the elegant, leafy suburb of Neuilly. Cross the river and you are in a mini-Manhattan that has grown since 1969 to become a mini-city in its own right.

The **Grande Arche** ❸❾ is further away than most of the towers, and only when you get close do you realise how big it is. A hollow cube 110m (360ft) high and 106m (347ft) wide, it could straddle the Champs-Élysées and tuck Notre-Dame underneath it. Built with remarkable speed (Danish architect Johann-Otto von Sprekelsen won the contest in 1983 and the arch was completed in time for the bicentennial of the French Revolution in 1989), the Grande Arche stands in line with the Arc de Triomphe and the Louvre. Its white gables are clad in Carrara marble, the outer facades in a combination of grey marble and glass. The two 'legs' contain offices, and the roof houses conference rooms and exhibition spaces. Increasing numbers of visitors and office workers have given rise to a growing number of shops, cinemas, hotels and restaurants at La Défense. Most are concentrated in the **Quatre Temps** shopping centre (www.les4temps.com), which also includes the 16-screen ugc Ciné Cité La Défense cinema complex (www.ugc.fr).

Across the main concourse, a 12m (39ft) bronze thumb by César literally sticks out like a sore thumb. Stroll down the tiers of terraces and you will discover even more statues, fountains and murals by Miró, Calder and other modern artists, all detailed on street-plans from the Espace Défense (15 place de la Défense; www.ladefense.fr). Here you can also find out about the history of the area and the new towers under construction, including Hermitage Plaza designed by Sir Norman

The Grande Arche at La Défense

Foster, which will be the tallest building in the European Union upon completion in 2018.

EXCURSIONS

VERSAILLES

Louis XIV's palace at **Versailles**  is as extravagant as the Sun King was himself. A visit to the château takes most or all of a day and entails a lot of walking. Versailles is 24km (15 miles) southwest of Paris, by road (N10), by train from Gare St-Lazare to Versailles-Rive Droite, or by RER (line C) to Versailles-Rive Gauche.

Palace: Tue–Sun 9am–5.30pm, Apr–Oct until 6.30pm. Marie Antoinette's Estate (incl. Petit Trianon) and Grand Trianon: Tue–Sun noon–5.30pm, Apr–Oct until 6.30pm. Gardens: daily Apr–Oct 8am–8.30pm (except when the musical extravaganzas

The Galerie des Glaces at Versailles

'Grandes Eaux Musicales' are held, see website for details), Nov–Mar 8am–6pm. Various ticket combinations are available on the website: www.chateauversailles.fr.

Highlights of the interior include: the baroque **Royal Chapel**; the **State Apartments**, in which Louis XIV entertained; the Salon de Diane, where he played billiards; the 73m (240ft) long **Galerie des Glaces** (Hall of Mirrors); and the King's Bedroom, where Louis died of gangrene in 1715. In the Queen's Bedroom, 19 royal children were born, the births often attended by members of the court, as was the custom.

The grandest facade faces west to the gardens, where the fountains spout to music at weekends (Apr–Oct). The **Grand Trianon**, the small palace Louis XIV used when he wanted to escape the vast château; the **Petit Trianon**, favoured by Louis XV and the **Hameau** and miniature farm are also worth a visit. The Hameau was built as a place of lesiure in a vernacular, rustic style by Louis XVI's queen, Marie-Antoinette, as was the fashion among the French aristocracy of the time. It provided a more intimate setting and an escape from some of the formality of court life.

FONTAINEBLEAU

The seat of sovereigns from Louis IX to Napoleon III and a glittering example of French Mannerism, the château at **Fontainebleau** 🐠 (www.musee-chateau-fontainebleau.fr; Wed–Mon 9.30am–5pm, Apr–Sept until 6pm, last admission 45 mins before closing; charge) makes a pleasant day trip from Paris. Here Louis XIV signed the Revocation of the Edict of Nantes in 1685, and Napoleon I signed his first act of abdication in 1814. More recently (1945–65) Fontainebleau was the headquarters of the military branch of NATO. Fontainebleau is 64km (40 miles) southeast of Paris by the A6 or by train from Gare de Lyon, then Ligne A bus to the château.

MALMAISON

Set in lovely grounds, the château at **Malmaison** ㊷ (www.chateau-almaison.fr; Wed–Mon Apr–Sept 10am–12.30pm, 1.30–5.45pm, Sat–Sun until 6.15pm, Oct–Mar 10am–12.30pm and 1.30–5.15pm, Sat–Sun until 5.45pm; charge) was the home of Napoleon's wife, Josephine, who continued to live here after their divorce. Many of her possessions are on display. Malmaison is 6km (4 miles) west of Paris. Métro: Grande Arche de La Défense, then bus 258, or RER to Rueil-Malmaison, followed by bus Optile 27.

VAUX-LE-VICOMTE

This 17th-century château (www.vaux-le-vicomte.com; mid-Mar–mid-Nov daily 10am–6pm, candlelit visits May–mid-Oct Sat 8pm–midnight; charge) was designed by Louis Le Vau, André Le Nôtre and Charles Le Brun for Louis XIV's finance minister, Fouquet. No sooner was it completed than the king had its owner arrested for embezzlement and jailed for life. **Vaux-le-Vicomte** ㊸ is 55km (35 miles) southeast of Paris on the N5 or by train from Gare de Lyon to Melun, then a taxi ride.

GIVERNY

Claude Monet lived at this house in **Giverny** ㊹ (www.fondation-monet.com; Apr–Oct daily 9.30am–6pm, last admission 5.30pm; charge) from 1883 to 1926 and painted the gardens many times, especially the water lilies (see the Musée de l'Orangerie, page 43). Giverny is situated 85km (53 miles) northwest of Paris by the A13, D181 and D5, or by train from Gare St-Lazare to Vernon, with a shuttle bus from the station to Giverny.

Châteaux day trips

Cityrama ParisVision (tel: 01 44 55 61 00; www.pariscity vision.com) runs day trips from Paris to Fontainebleau and Vaux-le-Vicomte (Wed–Mon Apr–Oct).

DISNEYLAND PARIS

Disneyland Paris ⁴⁵ (www.disneylandparis.com; daily, times vary but usually 10am-8pm, Studios Park usually 10am–6pm, longer opening hours in summer; charge) is an ambitious recreation complex that encompasses a theme park, hotels, restaurants, a convention centre, a golf course, tennis courts and several swimming pools; and attracts over 16 million visitors a year. In the theme park itself, Main Street USA recaptures the traditions of small-town America at the turn of the 20th century, and

The original Japanese bridge in Monet's garden

leads to four other 'lands' – Frontierland, Adventureland, Fantasyland and Discoveryland. Each themed section has a variety of fun experiences to offer. Every day at 7pm there is a parade including floats inspired by the famous Disney movies. In the **Walt Disney Studios Park** visitors can explore film sets; the Twilight Zone Tower of Terror thrill ride ends with a sheer drop into a black hole.

The resort is 32km (20 miles) east of Paris, near Marne-la-Vallée. A motorway gives access from the city and the airports, Charles-de-Gaulle and Orly. Speedy commuter trains (RER line A) from the capital and even faster long-distance trains (TGV) serve Marne-la-Vallée/Chessy station near the entrance.

WHAT TO DO

Critics of Paris sometimes dismiss it as a 'museum city', a conglomeration too reverently preserved in aspic. Nothing could be further from the truth. The past matters, but this is also one of the liveliest and most influential cultural power-houses in the world, with an enormous army of contemporary creators and outlets for film, theatre, music and fashion. It's also a consumer paradise, with some of the best shops you'll find anywhere.

SHOPPING

The range of shops in Paris is vast. There are the eye-poppingly expensive jewellers on elegant place Vendôme, the high fashion icons in formerly literary St-Germain-des-Prés, the much-loved book stalls on the banks of the Seine, and the ever-popular flea markets on the edges of the city. There's also an enduring tradition of small, special-ist retailers.

WHAT TO BUY WHERE

Each neighbourhood has its own mood and atmosphere, and the shops often reflect its history and the people who live there. In terms of fashion, expect boho design-ers in Montmartre; designer couture on rue du Fau-bourg-St-Honoré and avenue Montaigne; and cool, con-temporary streetwear around

Gourmet paradise

Paris is a famously foodie city, and every *quartier* has its *chocolatiers*, superb *pâtisseries* and *boulangeries* (bakers), *boucheries* (butchers), delicatessens, ripe-smelling *fromageries* (cheese shops) and bustling street markets.

Items for sale at the Marché de St-Ouen

Ultra-trendy Merci concept store in the Marais

rue Etienne-Marcel. The exclusive western sector of the 7th *arrondissement* is good for traditional menswear along with upmarket interior design boutiques. Chic place Vendôme glitters with diamond-encrusted baubles, but you will find more original pieces in St-Germain-des-Prés or the Marais. Opulent antiques are sold around quai Voltaire in the 7th and rue du Faubourg-St-Honoré in the 8th. Retro furnishing and ceramics from the 1960s and '70s are popular near Bastille and Montmartre.

That said, the shopping map of Paris is far from static, reflecting an ebb and flow that goes with the rise and fall of different areas. The Champs-Élysées, which zigzagged from the epitome of glamour in the early 20th century to that of tourist dross in the 1980s, started returning to favour in the 1990s, and is now buzzing with upmarket brands including multi-brand store LE66. Long-staid rue St-Honoré is now the focus for a more avant-garde fashion set, chasing trends at concept store Colette. Similarly, designer fashion has migrated to once-literary St-Germain-des-Prés, to the chagrin of those who bemoan the disappearance of favourite bookshops and food stores.

Since the 1990s, restoration of its beautiful *hôtels particuliers* and the installation of several important museums have transformed the Marais into a highly international district with youthful fashion boutiques and cutting-edge design shops. Rue Charlot, in the 3rd, is a hive of contemporary fashion activity, while the hub of the Marais's gay area around rue Vieille-du-Temple has gay-oriented bookshops and clothing stores.

Some neighbourhoods reflect the changing population of Paris. In the 13th *arrondissement,* with its large South-East Asian population, you'll find Chinese supermarkets and *pâtisseries* among the high-rise tower blocks. Another overlooked corner over in the 10th, the Canal St-Martin has now resolutely made its mark on the retail map, with the three kitsch and colourful shops of quirky fashion retailer Antoine et Lili.

Other areas have not fared as well: the aristocratic past of boulevards Bonne Nouvelle and Montmartre is a distant memory smudged by discount stores and fast-food chains. Forum des Halles, right in the heart of the city, is the epitome of retail decline, with its three-level underground shopping mall long reviled (but no less crowded) for its array of brash chain stores and strong whiff of juvenile delinquency. However, a huge regeneration project is due to replace the ugly 1970s Forum with a new blend of park and shopping centre, partially sheltered by a massive green glass canopy. Although the project is already years behind schedule (it was originally due for completion in 2012), it could well bring yet another reversal of fortune.

The daily market on rue Mouffetard

MARKETS

The city's markets pull in bargain hunters, gourmets and collectors alike. There are three fleamarkets: on the outskirts, the classy Marché de St-Ouen, largest in the world, the smaller Marché de Vanves, and, in the 12th *arrondissement*, the Marché d'Aligre. 'Roving' street markets are held two or three mornings a week (7am–2.30pm); at these you can find authentic produce and a distinctive local character.

In addition there are over 50 street markets; some have just a few stalls, whereas others, such as Marché Bastille or avenue Daumesnil, stretch for hundreds of metres and have a superb range of stock. Market streets, including rue Mouffetard, in the Latin Quarter, have food shops with stalls that spill onto the pavement and are open all day from Tuesday to Saturday, with a long break for lunch, and on Sunday morning. For a full list with opening times, see http://marches.equipements.paris.fr.

SPORTS

The city caters fairly well for the sports enthusiast. You can find details on sporting events in the Wednesday edition of *Le Figaro*. For comprehensive information (in French) on sporting facilities, visit www.paris.fr.

SPECTATOR SPORTS

Football and rugby fans can watch games at the huge **Stade de France** (rue Francis de Pressensé, St-Denis; www.stadefrance.com) just north of the city ringroad. The **Parc des Princes** (22 rue du Commandant Guilbaud, 75016; www.leparcdesprinces.fr) is home to Paris's premier division football team, Paris St-Germain. The huge **Palais Omnisports Paris Bercy** (8 boulevard de Bercy, 75012; www.bercy.fr) hosts events including ice-skating, motor sports, basketball and tennis.

For horse racing, the Grand Prix de l'Arc de Triomphe takes place in October, at **Longchamp** in the Bois de Boulogne.

PARTICIPANT SPORTS

The few public tennis courts in Paris, such as those at the Jardin du Luxembourg, are available on a first-come-first-served basis. Municipal swimming pools include the **Piscine Josephine Baker**, which floats on the Seine and has a retractable roof for warm weather. For details of municipal sports facilities, see www.paris.fr. The quais de Seine, Bois de Boulogne and Canal St-Martin offer good cycling opportunities; the **Fédération Française de Cyclotourisme**, www.ffct.org, has details of cycling clubs.

Sporting events

Major sporting events include the Six Nations Cup in Feb/March, the Marathon in April, and the French Tennis Open in May/June at the Stade Roland-Garros.

ENTERTAINMENT

For event listings, buy one of the weekly guides, *Pariscope* or *L'Officiel des Spectacles* – issued on Wednesday. The Wednesday supplement of *Le Figaro* is another good source. Up-to-date information can also be found at www.parisinfo.com.

THEATRE

The main national theatre is the **Comédie Française** (1 place Colette, 75001; www.comedie-francaise.fr), where works by such revered writers as Molière and Racine are performed. Modern classics are shown here and at the **Théâtre du Vieux Colombier** (21 rue du Vieux-Colombier, 75006; www.comedie-francaise.fr); the **Théâtre du Châtelet** (2 rue Edouard Colonne, 75001, www.chatelet-theatre.com) hosts opera, classical concerts and the occasional ballet.

OPERA AND BALLET

Opera and ballet are staged in the lavish **Palais Garnier** (place de l'Opéra) and in the modern **Opéra Bastille** (2bis place de la Bastille). www.operadeparis.fr.

CINEMA

Paris has numerous multi-screen cinemas showing the latest blockbusters, but if you would rather see a French classic, there are dozens of good art-house cinemas too. Most cinemas in the centre of Paris show films in their original language with sub-titles in French ('VO' – *version originale*). For a unique cinematic experience visit **La Pagode** (57bis rue de Babylone, 75007; www.etoile-cinemas.com/pagode), where the latest films are shown in an exotic Japanese setting complete with a tea room. Cinema buffs can also pay homage at the **Cinémathèque Française** (51 rue de Bercy, 75012, www.cinematheque.fr) in a Cubist building by Frank Gehry.

JAZZ, POP AND ROCK

Paris has excellent jazz credentials and a long list of clubs. An established venue is the **Caveau de la Huchette** (5 rue de la Huchette, 75005; www.caveau delahuchette.fr). **Le Sunset/ Sunside** (60 rue des Lombards, 75001; www.sunset-sunside. com) is two jazz clubs in one: electric jazz and world music, plus acoustic. Bigger names perform at **New Morning** (7 rue des Petites-Ecuries, 75010; www.newmorning.com) and the Jazz Club Etoile (Le Méridien,

Cinémathèque Française

81 boulevard Gouvion-St-Cyr, 75017; www.jazzclub-paris.com).

Pop and rock concerts are held at the **Zénith** in the Parc de la Villette (see page 65), the **Stade de France**, Parc des Princes and the **Palais Omnisports** Paris Bercy (see page 95). Ticket offices *(billeteries)* at branches of the Fnac chain (www.fnac.com) or Virgin Megastore (www.virginmegastore. fr) on the Champs-Élysées will have details of who is playing.

CABARETS

Lavish nearly-nude cabarets, geared mainly for tourists, hark back to the capital's 'naughty' image of yesteryear. The **Lido** (116bis av. des Champs-Élysées, 75008; www.lido.fr) and the **Folies Bergère** (32 rue Richer, 75009; www.foliesbergere.com) are classic survivors. Newer **Crazy Horse** (12 av. George V, 75008; www.lecrazyhorseparis.com) puts on slick yet knowingly tongue-in-cheek shows. The celebrated **Moulin Rouge** (82 blvd de Clichy, 75018; www.moulinrouge.fr) puts on two shows a night.

Cool hangout Café Charbon

CLUBS AND BARS

The words 'Paris nightlife' make many visitors think of Montmartre and Montparnasse, but these days the biggest after-dark buzz is around rue Oberkampf in the east of the city. **Café Charbon** (109 rue Oberkampf, 75011; www.nouveau casino.net) launched the area's nightlife boom two decades ago, and is still going strong; behind it is the same management's **Nouveau Casino** one of the liveliest nightclubs in the city. Nearby **L'Alimentation Générale** (64 rue Jean-Pierre Timbaud, 75011; www.alimentation-generale.net) is a cavernous bar with club nights and world music concerts.

Exciting venues are not confined to the east. **Showcase** (Pont Alexandre III, 75008; www.showcase.fr) is a gorgeous club underneath the Right Bank end of the Pont Alexandre III, which attracts a trendy young crowd.

In the centre of town, film director David Lynch has set up the city's first members' bar, the very swanky and atmospheric

Club Silencio (142 rue Montmartre, 75002; www.silencio-club.com); non-members can get in after midnight. Another big-name central drinking den is **Harry's Bar** (5 rue Daunou, 75002; www.harrys-bar.fr). Hemingway, Gershwin and others frequented this authentic Paris institution. The cocktails are excellent – and strong.

Further north, and with a more youthful, electro vibe, is **Point Ephémère** (200 quai de Valmy, 75010; www.pointephemere.org), set on the bank of the Canal St-Martin a short walk southwest from Jaurès Métro station. This expansive clubbing and concert venue also has a good restaurant and café, a waterfront terrace in summer, and a gallery.

The Marais is the place to go for the gay scene, with institutions like Raidd (23 rue du Temple, 75004; www.raiddbar.com) and **Café Cox** (15 rue des Archives, 75004; www.cox.fr), or the rue des Ecouffes, peppered with lesbian bars, cafés and boutiques.

For information about clubs and concerts, pick up the free, fortnightly pocket magazine *Lylo* (www.lylo.fr) in trendy bars and music shops.

CHILDREN

For most children, Disneyland (see page 89) will appeal far more than city sightseeing. For a cheaper alternative, an afternoon in one of Paris's parks (see pages 41 and 75) might do the trick. For small children there are merry-go-rounds, puppet theatres (not Jul–Aug), pony rides and toy boats in the **Jardin du Luxembourg**. The **Jardin d'Acclimatation** (see page 61) is a children's park with a zoo, pony rides and puppet shows in the Bois de Boulogne. For the scientifically minded, there is a lot to learn in the **Cité des Sciences et de l'Industrie** (see page 65), where the Cité des Enfants is aimed at children aged 2–12. Kids can also get hands on with science at the **Palais de la Découverte** (see page 56) on the Champs-Élysées.

CALENDAR OF EVENTS

For details of these and other events, see www.parisinfo.com.

January Chinese New Year, Chinatown. Métro: Porte d'Ivry.

Spring Foire du Trône (late March–early May), a monster funfair at Pelouse de Reuilly, Bois de Vincennes, Métro: Porte Dorée.

April Paris Marathon ends on the Champs-Élysées.

Good Friday The Archbishop of Paris leads Procession of the Cross up the steps of Sacré-Cœur basilica, Montmartre, Métro: Anvers.

May/June French Open Tennis Championships, chic Grand Slam event, Roland-Garros stadium, Métro: Porte d'Auteuil.

June For the Fête de la Musique (Music Festival) on the 21st, there are free concerts all over Paris.

July Bastille Day (14th). Festivities include a military parade along the Champs-Élysées, a firework display at the Trocadéro and dancing on place de la Bastille. The Tour de France ends on the Champs-Élysées. Paris Cinéma, international film festival, screenings at various venues; see www.paris-cinema.org. Night-time firework displays and illuminated fountains at the Château de Versailles (mid-July–mid-Sept).

July/August Paris-Plages, the wildly successful 'city beach' brings sand, palm trees and a host of open-air attractions and entertainment to the banks of river and canal for four weeks. See www.paris.fr.

September Journées du Patrimoine, open days at otherwise off-limits government and private buildings.

October Prix de l'Arc de Triomphe, France's biggest horse race, Longchamp, Bois de Boulogne, Métro: Porte d'Auteuil and free shuttle-bus. Festival d'Automne, the annual festival of theatre, music and dance (until December). Nuit Blanche, museums and cultural venues open late on the first Saturday of the month, with special events laid on. See www.paris.fr.

November The arrival of Beaujolais Nouveau (third Tuesday of the month) is celebrated in bars and restaurants.

December Christmas markets, La Défense and Champs-Élysées. Notre-Dame is packed for 11pm Christmas Eve Mass. New Year's Eve crowds pour onto the Champs-Élysées, and there are fireworks at the Trocadéro.

EATING OUT

Paris is considered one of the culinary capitals of the world, and deservedly so. In the 2000s, the French capital's dining scene was criticised for being slow to evolve, unlike other competitors on the international stage. Such concerns have been more or less neutralised by the steady rise of regional and international cuisines, the runaway success of a number of young owner-chefs, often working in tiny or canteen-style premises, and by the local 'fooding' trend and global slow food movement.

The downside is that eating out in Paris is more expensive than ever, and good bargain bistro fare – the sort of thing visitors to Paris used to rave about on their return home – is harder to find. Consult the list of recommendations in this guide (see page 108) and get the lowdown on the latest new

The Louvre's elegant Café Marly

Chez Prune, great for tapas and people-watching

openings in the free weekly guide *A Nous Paris* (www.anous.fr), available on Mondays in Métro stations.

CLASSIC TO CONTEMPORARY

The great cuisines of the world can be counted on one hand, and French cuisine is one of them. What the term implies is an established, coherent body of ingredients, techniques and dishes, which have all been developed, studied and perfected by masters of the art over many years.

This is not to say that French food isn't evolving. New flavours are integrated into the cooking all the time, albeit carefully. Curry, lime, peppers, coconut and lemongrass are all fairly common ingredients on gastronomic menus. Most dishes remain French at the core, but exotic nuances are certainly part of the high-end experience. In the middle ground, couscous is eaten almost as often as *bœuf bourguignon*, and sushi seems to be the city's favourite fast food.

Even in terms of technique, French cooking has modernised; sauces and pastries, for example, tend to be lighter than they were previously, and vegetables are more prevalent. Menus have been simplified and better aligned to contemporary appetites.

The advantage of this from a visitor's perspective is that the classic dishes we dream about can still be found in authentic form on French tables. If you want French onion soup, you can find it. If you order *steak au poivre*, out will come that desired slab of beef in a creamy, peppery sauce that spills across the plate towards your crispy pile of *frites*.

Another thing that makes French food extraordinary (and the bad French food, on a gracious day, forgivable) is the degree to which it is social. Even with the increased pace of modern life, the French still believe in sitting down and sharing meals in good company over a bottle of wine – so much so, indeed, that one of the most prominent fashions in recent years has been for canteen-style restaurants where diners rub up together on plain wooden benches seated at long communal tables. After all, food in France is much more than just sustenance.

WHERE TO EAT
Bistros tend to serve simple, traditional dishes. The food quality varies from one to the next, unlike the menus, which are practically carbon copies of one another: potato and herring

LE FOODING

The term 'Le Fooding', coined in 1999 by journalist Alexandre Cammas, joins the two English words 'food' and 'feeling' to express an attitude towards dining that emphasises emotion, atmosphere, alluring food presentation, imagination, entertainment and time, as much as high-quality food on the plate. Says Cammas, 'People need a lot more than just good food to feel well fed.' It's all about approaching the table with the mind and all the senses, not just an empty belly and a greedy tongue. In a way, this is what France has always been famous for. For restaurants that share these ideals, visit www.lefooding.com.

Tipping

A service charge of 12 to 15 percent is, by law, included in the price given at restaurants, bars and cafés, so in theory you don't have to tip. However, it is polite when paying for drinks to round up the total and to leave one to five euros after a meal, depending on the quality of the service and the restaurant concerned.

salad, duck confit, beef daube, chocolate mousse and tarte Tatin are a few of the classic dishes. Brasseries (the louder, brighter, Belle Epoque option) often offer similar fare, but also specialise in seafood – heaps of oysters, mussels, langoustines, lobsters and clams spinning past on waiters' dexterous palms – and Alsatian dishes such as choucroute.

Standard, everyday cafés usually serve sandwiches, notably the classic *croque-monsieur* (grilled ham and cheese) and a variety of salads. However, modern cafés – trendy, chic establishments that pack in fashionable crowds – serve full menus, typically of contemporary, cosmopolitan food with a Mediterranean bent, and often at prices to match full-blown restaurants.

FINE DINING

At the high end, Michelin-starred restaurants range from being gloriously old-fashioned, with truffle-studded foie gras terrines and venison in grand old sauces, to being acrobatically cutting-edge (at the time of printing Paris has nine restaurants with three stars). One of the best ways to enjoy such restaurants is to opt for the chef's tasting menu (*dégustation*), which gets you a host of dishes in smaller-than-usual portions. Quite a few of the top-notch addresses serve fixed lunch menus that are significantly cheaper than the à la carte options – but their popularity means you'll need to book weeks in advance. Getting a table at any currently fashionable restaurant, for that matter, can present the same challenge.

Generally speaking, restaurants serve lunch from noon to 2.30 or 3pm and dinner from around 7 or 8 to 10.30 or 11pm, although this may vary, particularly in August, when many places shut for the summer.

GLOBAL CUISINE

If you get to the point where you think you might burst if you look at another plate of French food, take a break at one of the city's international restaurants. Paris is especially good for food from Morocco, Thailand, Vietnam and Japan. The greatest concentration of Chinese and Vietnamese restaurants is in the 5th and 13th *arrondissements* (roughly speaking, the Latin Quarter and southeast to the new Left Bank), and Japanese restaurants are numerous in parts of the 1st (especially on and around rue Ste-Anne). The best

Les Cocottes serves its dishes in cast-iron pots, hence its name

The iconic Art Deco La Coupole

Moroccan restaurants are dotted across the capital, but the area around the Bastille is a good place to start. There is also excellent Lebanese food to be found in the 8th and 16th *arrondissements* (Madeleine, Grands Boulevards, Champs-Élysées and West).

EATING OUT WITH CHILDREN
Taking your children out to a restaurant should not be a problem, although you should check beforehand with the more upmarket places. French children are used to eating out from an early age, and are therefore generally well-behaved in restaurants. Many establishments offer a children's menu. If not, they may split a *prix fixe* menu between two. With very young children, just request an extra plate and give them food from your own. With the bread that should come automatically to a French table, and ice-cream or fruit to follow, most children will be well fed.

TO HELP YOU ORDER

Do you have a table? **Avez-vous une table?**

The bill, please **L'addition, s'il vous plaît**

I would like ... **J'aimerais...**

tea **du thé**	pepper **du poivre**
coffee **un café**	salad **de la salade**
milk **du lait**	soup **de la soupe**
sugar **du sucre**	fish **du poisson**
wine **du vin**	seafood **des fruits de mer**
beer **une bière**	
water **de l'eau**	meat **de la viande**
bread **du pain**	very rare **bleu**
butter **du beurre**	rare **saignant**
cheese **du fromage**	medium-rare **rose**
chips (fries) **des frites**	medium **à point**
salt **du sel**	well done **bien cuit**

MENU READER

agneau lamb	**huîtres** oysters
ail garlic	**jambon** ham
bœuf beef	**moules** mussels
canard duck	**œufs** eggs
champignons mushrooms	**oignons** onions
chou cabbage	**petits pois** peas
choufleur cauliflower	**poire** pear
crevettes roses/grises prawns/shrimps	**pomme** apple
	pomme de terre potato
dinde turkey	**porc** pork
épinards spinach	**poulet** chicken
escargots snails	**riz** rice
fraises strawberries	**saucisse** sausage
framboises raspberries	**saumon** salmon
haricots verts green beans	**thon** tuna

PLACES TO EAT

We have used the following symbols to give an idea of the price for a three-course meal for one, including half a bottle of house wine, tax and service:

€€€€ over 60 euros   €€ 25–50 euros
€€€ 40–60 euros   € under 25 euros

THE ISLANDS

Le Sergent Recruteur €€€€ *41 rue St-Louis-en-l'Ile, 75004; tel: 01 43 54 75 42;* www.lesergentrecruteur.fr. Closed Sun and Mon. Opened in 2012, this stylish restaurant in an ancient house has already gained a Michelin star. Chef Antonin Bonnet has worked in Provence, Asia and London and this eclectic mix can be felt in his food; there is even sake on the drinks menu. But the restaurant's main appeal is top-quality seasonal cuisine, cooked simply.

THE RIGHT BANK

LOUVRE AND TUILERIES

Le Fumoir €€€ *6 rue de l'Amiral-de-Coligny, 75001; tel: 01 42 92 00 24;* www.lefumoir.com. Open for lunch and dinner daily; brunch on Sunday. Facing the Louvre, spacious, sophisticated Le Fumoir is renowned for shaking some of the best cocktails in town. It serves light pan-European cooking, such as poached cod with a warm salad of fennel, tomatoes and olives.

Le Grand Véfour €€€€ *17 rue de Beaujolais, 75001; tel: 01 42 96 56 27;* www.grand-vefour.com. Open for lunch and dinner Mon–Fri. Set under the arches of the Palais-Royal, this is one of the most beautiful restaurants in Paris. Le Grand Véfour opened its doors in 1784 and has fed the likes of Emperor Napoleon and writers Alphonse Lamartine and Victor Hugo. Today it serves haute cuisine in the hands of chef Guy Martin.

Café Marly €€€€ *Palais du Louvre, 93 rue de Rivoli, 75001; tel: 01 49 26 06 60;* www.cafe-marly.com. Open for breakfast, lunch and dinner daily until 2am. Rest from your labours at the Louvre in the lavish Second Empire-style rooms facing the Pyramid, or on the attractive covered terrace. The food is modern European, the service sometimes a bit slow.

THE GRANDS BOULEVARDS

Chartier € *7 rue du Faubourg-Montmartre, 75009; tel: 01 47 70 86 29;* www.bouillon-chartier.com. Open for lunch and dinner daily; arrive before 1pm or before 8pm at night or you may not get a seat. The ambience at this historic budget option is an experience in itself: Belle Epoque decor, snappy waiters, shared tables and plenty of bonhomie.

L'Opéra €€€€ *Palais Garnier, entrance on place Jacques Rouché, 75009; tel: 01 42 68 86 80;* www.opera-restaurant.fr. Open 8am–midnight daily. With its two-storey undulating glass front, space-age interior with bright red chairs and carpets and, most of all, its location inside the Palais Garnier – the first time a restaurant has been set up here – this is one of the most talked-about restaurants in Paris. Splash out on roast and poached guinea fowl served with carrot and sesame salad, or slide up to the bar for one of the sumptuous cocktails.

Café de la Paix €€€€ *5 place de l'Opéra, 75009; tel: 01 40 07 36 36;* www.cafedelapaix.fr. Open for breakfast, lunch and dinner daily. Its prices are steep, but this is one of the city's most historic cafés (it opened in 1862), and it is convenient for the Palais Garnier opposite and the department stores on boulevard Haussmann. There is a family-friendly brunch on Sundays.

Spring €€€€ *6 rue Bailleul, 75001; 01 45 96 05 72;* www.spring paris.fr. Open for dinner Tue–Sat. Young Chicago-born chef Daniel Rose is the talk of the town. His small restaurant books out months in advance, and with good reason; even haughty French critics have been bowled over. The superb seasonal cuisine is put together in an open kitchen, with the chatty Rose presiding; there's a wine bar downstairs that you don't have to book for. This is one of the best restaurants in Paris.

Willi's Wine Bar €€€ *13 rue des Petits-Champs, 75001; tel: 01 42 61 05 09*; www.williswinebar.com. Open for lunch and dinner, Mon–Sat. In business for over 30 years, this classy establishment near the Palais Garnier is great for a full-blown meal à table or simply a glass of wine at its high oak bar.

BEAUBOURG, MARAIS, BASTILLE AND EAST

L'As du Fallafel € *34 rue des Rosiers, 75004; tel: 01 48 87 63 60.* Open noon–midnight Sun–Fri. The best *falafel* in Paris is a meal in itself. There are also *shawarma* sandwiches in pitta bread. Great location in the heart of the Marais.

Brasserie Bofinger €€€€ *5–7 rue de la Bastille, 75004; tel: 01 42 72 87 82* www.bofingerparis.com. Open for lunch and dinner daily. Close to the Opéra Bastille, the huge (300-seater) Bofinger is the archetypal Belle Epoque brasserie, complete with lush red-and-gold decor. It is a great place in which to enjoy delicious oysters and seafood, and specialities from Alsace such as *choucroute*.

Chai 33 €€€ *33 cour St-Emilion, 75012; tel: 01 53 44 01 01*; www.chai33.com. Open for lunch and dinner daily. This restaurant is set in a light, airy former wine warehouse with a view of Bercy park. Choose your wine according to six styles, from light with a bite to rich and silky, with refreshing fusion food to match. Unpretentious *sommeliers* are on hand to help with wine choices.

Le Chateaubriand €€€€ *129 avenue Parmentier, 75011; tel: 01 43 57 45 95.* Open for dinner only Tue–Sat. The latest food sensation in Paris is the 'néo-bistrot', run by young chefs creating innovative, cosmopolitan cuisine for usually less than €50 per head. This one has been voted one of the top 20 best restaurants in the world. Daily changing menu. Book well in advance.

Chez Omar €€ *47 rue de Bretagne, 75003; tel: 01 42 72 36 26.* Open for lunch Mon–Sat, for dinner daily. Couscous is one of the most popular international dishes in Paris, and this perennially popular address does some of the best. It doesn't take bookings, so get there early or join the queue of fashionable people outside. The portions are hearty, and the roast lamb is superb.

Chez Prune €€ *36 rue Beaurepaire, 75010; tel: 01 42 41 30 47.* Open for lunch and dinner daily. This is a cornerstone of the trendy Canal St-Martin area, and a great spot from which to watch the world go by. Good food at lunchtime; tapas-style snacks at night.

Le Petit Fer à Cheval €€ *30 rue Vieille-du-Temple, 75004; tel: 01 42 72 47 47.* Open for lunch and dinner daily. With its tiny horseshoe-shaped bar, this café on the Marais's trendy rue Vieille-du-Temple, is atmospheric and a great favourite with the bourgeois-bohemian crowd. Decent food. Friendly service.

Saveurs Végét'Halles €€ *41 rue des Bourdonnais, 75001; tel: 01 40 41 93 95;* www.saveursvegethalles.fr. Open Mon–Sat for lunch and dinner. Good-value vegetarian and vegan restaurant south east of Les Halles. The menu includes salads, mushroom roast with blackberry and ginger sauce and there is a good choice of desserts such as fruit crumble or chocolate and banana cake.

Le Square Trousseau €€€ *1 rue Antoine-Vollon, 75012; tel: 01 43 43 06 00;* www.squaretrousseau.com. Open for breakfast, lunch and dinner daily. A spacious bistro with Art Deco lamps, colourful tiles, a glamorous bar and terrace facing a leafy square. Among the delights available are gazpacho, tuna tartare, rosemary lamb and spring vegetables, beef with shallot sauce, and raspberry gratin.

Le Train Bleu €€€€ *Gare de Lyon, 75012; tel: 01 43 43 09 06;* www.le-train-bleu.com. Open for lunch and dinner daily. Built over a century ago, this huge restaurant in the Gare de Lyon is an artistic marvel, with frescoed ceilings and Belle Epoque murals. Classic French dishes are efficiently served. Good-value set menus.

CHAMPS-ÉLYSÉES AND TROCADÉRO

Alain Ducasse au Plaza Athénée €€€€ *25 avenue Montaigne, 75008; tel: 01 53 67 65 00;* www.alain-ducasse.com. Open for lunch Thu–Fri, dinner Mon–Fri. Here, cooking has been elevated to an art form, by France's first recipient of six Michelin stars (three apiece for two restaurants, although Alain Ducasse au Plaza Athénée currently holds only two stars). Expect truffles in abundance and superb vegetables from Provence. Reserve well ahead.

L'Entredgeu €€ *83 rue Laugier, 75017; tel: 01 40 54 97 24.* Open for lunch and dinner Tue–Sat. The unpronounceable name and non-central location apart, this superior bistro has a lot going for it. Dishes include roast duckling in honey sauce and lots of foie gras, and the decor is suitably cosy and intimate.

Le Pavillon Elysée Lenôtre €€€ *10 avenue des Champs-Élysées,* 75008; tel: 01 42 65 85 10; www.lenotre.com. Open for lunch and dinner Mon–Sat. This pâtisserie is opposite the Grand Palais, in a glass pavilion created for the 1900 World Fair. The main reason to come here is for the delicious cakes, for which Lenôtre is best known. It's also possible to have a three-course meal.

WESTERN PARIS

Guy Savoy €€€€ *18 rue Troyon, 75017; tel: 01 43 80 40 61;* www. guysavoy.com. Open for lunch Tue–Fri, dinner Tue–Sat. The son of a gardener, Guy Savoy has an obsession with vegetables that has anticipated the current trend by more than a decade. The Michelin-starred chef happily pairs truffles with lentils or artichokes, and regularly makes the rounds to greet his guests.

Pré Catelan €€€€ *route de Suresnes, 75016; tel: 01 44 14 41 14;* www.restaurant-precatelan.com. Open for lunch and dinner Tue–Sat, lunch only on Sun. This is one of the most romantic spots in Paris, situated in the heart of the Bois de Boulogne. Haute cuisine, centring on fresh truffles, lobster, lamb and fresh seafood. Book well ahead.

MONTMARTRE AND THE NORTHEAST

Chez Toinette €€€ *20 rue Germain-Pilon, 75018; tel: 01 42 54 44 36.* Open for dinner Mon–Sat. With its red walls and romantic lighting, this cosy and convivial bistro in the heights of Montmartre is a good bet for a classic French dinner. Try the wild boar terrine, and don't miss the superb crème brûlée.

Le Coq Rico €€€€ *98 rue Lepic, 75018; tel: 01 42 59 82 89;* www. lecoqrico.com. Open daily for lunch and dinner. If you love poultry then this smart restaurant from Antoine Westermann is the place to come. Try roast chicken accompanied by homemade chips. The plat du jour (€15) changes daily.

Rose Bakery €€ *46 rue des Martyrs, 75009; tel: 01 42 82 12 80.* Open for breakfast and lunch, Tue–Sun. Considered a folly when it opened in 2002, this deli-style café run by a Franco-British couple quickly made its mark, and is still going strong. The ingredients are of the highest quality, and make the soups, salads and quiches really shine. Vegetarian options.

THE LEFT BANK

LATIN QUARTER AND ST-GERMAIN-DES-PRÉS

L'Alcazar €€€ *62 rue Mazarine, 75006; tel: 01 53 10 19 99; www. alcazar.fr.* Open for lunch and dinner daily. Sir Terence Conran's contribution to the Paris restaurant scene was to transform this former music hall into a designer brasserie. It's been a hit, thanks to the easy-going atmosphere and competitively priced menu, which includes an upmarket interpretation of British fish and chips. DJs play on the mezzanine Wed–Sat.

L'Atelier de Joël Robuchon €€€€ *5 rue Montalembert, 75007; tel: 01 42 22 56 56; www.joel-robuchon.net.* Open for lunch and dinner daily. Parisians queue up in all weathers to sample the warm *brochettes de foie gras*, or tapenade with fresh tuna conjured by France's most revered chef. The two-star Michelin restaurant is set around an open kitchen, so you can watch the masters at work. A second Atelier can be found at Publicis Drugstore (www.publicisdrugstore.com) on the Champs-Élysées featuring set lunch menus. Gluten-free menu also available.

Le Comptoir €€€ *Hôtel Le Relais St-Germain, 9 carrefour de l'Odéon, 75006; tel: 01 44 27 07 97; www.hotel-paris-relais-saint-germain.com.* Open for breakfast, lunch and dinner daily. Since its launch in 2005, chef Yves Camdeborde's Art Deco restaurant – in the 17th-century hotel he runs with his wife Claudine – has been a steady hit with the city's gastronomes. Queues at lunchtime say all you need to know about the superb updated brasserie fare, such as chicken basquaise or salmon croque-monsieur. Tables are tightly packed, and the atmosphere is always convivial. You'll need to book months ahead for the set menu dinner.

La Ferrandaise €€€ *8 rue de Vaugirard, 75006; tel: 01 43 26 36 36; www.laferrandaise.com.* Open for lunch and dinner Mon–Fri, dinner only Sat. An old-fashioned red entrance sets the tone for this Left Bank restaurant, with its three atmospheric dining rooms boasting exposed beams and tiled floors. The food is traditional French: try the sardines cooked in lemon juice or the succulent Bresse chicken with morille mushrooms.

Polidor €€ *41 rue Monsieur-le-Prince, 75006; tel: 01 43 26 95 34; www.polidor.com.* Open for lunch and dinner daily. This bohemian restaurant is a perennial favourite of students and budget diners. The *plats du jour* have been reliable for around 150 years and arrive in hearty helpings. Bœuf bourguignon and tarte tatin are just the kind of traditional dishes to expect here.

Le Rostand €€€ *6 place Edmond-Rostand, 75006; tel: 01 43 54 61 58.* Open 8am–2am daily. This is one of the city's more upmarket cafés, with prices to match – but it's the sort of place you should treat yourself to at least once on a trip to Paris. A fine view of the Jardin du Luxembourg, good cocktails, a delicious snacks menu and an attractive mirrors-and-mahogany interior make this a classy spot for refreshment.

AROUND THE EIFFEL TOWER

Au Bon Accueil €€€€ *14 rue de Monttessuy, 75007; tel: 01 47 05 46 11; www.aubonaccueilparis.com.* Open for lunch and dinner Mon–Fri. This elegant bistro serves modern classics. The prix-fixe dinner menu (around €35) is viewed by many locals as one of the best deals in the neighbourhood, and the wine list is excellent. Seats on the terrace have views of its near neighbour the Eiffel Tower.

Les Cocottes €€€ *135 rue St-Dominique, 75007; www.maison-constant.com.* Open for lunch and dinner daily. This contemporary bistro run by chef Christian Constant has been packing Parisians in for its non-stop service of affordable and hearty grub: things like pumpkin soup or preserved shoulder of lamb. The name alludes to the cast-iron pots the food comes to the table in. No reservations.

Le Jules Verne €€€€ *2nd floor, Eiffel Tower, 75007; tel: 01 45 55 61 44; www.lejulesverne-paris.com. Open for lunch and dinner daily.* Location-wise, this restaurant on the second level of the Eiffel Tower is perfect for a celebration or romantic dinner, and since Alain Ducasse took over the nine-year concession in 2007, the food has improved considerably. Specialities include pan-seared turbot with violet artichokes and Provençal figs.

MONTPARNASSE

La Closerie des Lilas €€€€ *171 boulevard du Montparnasse, 75006; tel: 01 40 51 34 50; www.closeriedeslilas.fr. Open for lunch and dinner daily.* This historic brasserie still has a lot of charm and richly satisfying fare, though it lives off its reputation as a watering hole in the 1920s – tables are inscribed with the names of clients Lenin, Modigliani and André Breton. A pianist plays in the evening.

La Coupole €€€ *102 boulevard du Montparnasse, 75014; tel: 01 43 20 14 20; www.lacoupole-paris.com. Open for breakfast, lunch and dinner daily.* Opened in 1927, this vast, iconic Art Deco brasserie, now run by the Flo Brasserie group, is still going strong. Brasserie fare includes huge platters of shellfish and grilled meats.

A-Z TRAVEL TIPS

A Summary of Practical Information

ACCOMMODATION (see also Hotel Listings on page 133)
Paris is a popular destination all year round, so booking in advance is always recommended, especially from May to September and during the two annual fashion weeks. Most hotels stay open in the quieter months, but booking ahead is still a good idea, as many establishments offer discounts or package deals. A complete list of hotels is available from the Paris tourist information office.

For a long stay you might consider renting a serviced apartment; a list of addresses can be found at www.cityzenbooking.com. Travel sections of national newspapers carry advertisements; the *International Herald Tribune* and fusac (France-USA Contacts), available at expatriate hangouts and embassies, list accommodation for rent. **Alcôve & Agapes** (tel: 01 44 85 06 05; www.bed-and-breakfast-in-paris.com) organise rooms in private homes.

Do you have a single/double room? **Avez-vous une chambre pour une/deux personnes?**
What's the rate per night? **Quel est le prix pour une nuit?**

AIRPORTS
Paris has two main international airports. **Roissy-Charles-de-Gaulle (CDG)**, 30km (19 miles) northeast, and **Orly (ORY)**, 18km (11 miles) south. For information on both, see www.aeroportsdeparis.fr.
Charles-de-Gaulle to Central Paris
Train: The quickest way to central Paris from Roissy is by RER (line B) train. These leave roughly every 10–15 minutes between 5am and 11pm from station CDG 1 (for Terminal 1 and 3) and station CDG 2 (for Terminal 2) and run to the Métro stations at Gare du Nord and Châtelet. The journey takes about 30 minutes. Tickets cost €9.50; the five-zone RATP Navigo pass is valid.

Bus: Roissybus runs to rue Scribe (near the Palais Garnier) from terminals 1, 2A-2C, 2D-2B, 2E-2F and 3 (bus station). The service runs every 15–20 minutes from 5.45am to 11pm and takes 45–60 minutes. Tickets cost €10; the five-zone RATP Navigo pass is valid. Alternatively, the Air France bus runs to Charles-de-Gaulle-Etoile and Porte Maillot Métro stations and leaves from terminals 2A-2C (gate C2), 2D–2B (gate B1), 2E-2F (gate E8 or F9). It runs every 30 minutes from 5.45am to 11pm. Tickets cost €17.

Taxi: Can take anything from 30 minutes to over an hour. Fares are metered, with supplements charged for each large piece of luggage; expect to pay in the region of €50.

Orly to Central Paris

Train: Take the shuttle bus from gate F at Orly Sud or arrivals gate G at Orly Ouest to RER station Pont de Rungis (line C). Trains stop at St-Michel Notre-Dame and Champ de Mars Tour Eiffel, and run every 15 minutes from 5am to 11.30pm. The journey takes around 30 minutes. Tickets cost €2.50 for the bus and €3.95 for the RER; the four-zone RATP Navigo pass is valid. Alternatively, take the Orlyval shuttle train from gate K at Orly Sud or departure gate A at Orly Ouest to RER station Antony (line B). Trains stop at St Michel Notre-Dame, Châtelet Les Halles and Gare du Nord. Orlyval services run every seven minutes from 6am to 11pm; the RER every 15 minutes. Journey time is about 30 minutes. A combined ticket costs €11.30, or €8.70 with a three-zone RATP Navigo pass.

Bus: The Orlybus runs to Métro Denfert-Rochereau from Orly Sud gate G or Orly Ouest arrivals gate D. It runs every 10–20 minutes from 6am to midnight. The trip takes around 30 minutes, and tickets cost €7.20; the four-zone RATP Navigo pass is valid.

Air France buses to Montparnasse, Invalides and Etoile leave from Orly Sud gate L, or Orly Ouest arrivals gate C. They run every 20 minutes from 6am to 11.40pm and take an hour. Tickets cost €12.

Taxi: The journey from Orly to the city centre takes 20–40 minutes; expect to pay in the region of €40.

BICYCLE HIRE (RENTAL)

Cycling in Paris has been revolutionised by the city council's hugely successful Vélib' scheme (www.velib.paris.fr), launched in 2007. Vélib' lets you pick up and return one of over 20,000 bikes at any of 1,800 automated 'stations' all over the city. A card valid for a week or a day can be bought from the stations, or online in advance. You then pay for each journey you make, according to its duration; trips under 30 minutes are free.

Alternatively, you can hire bikes and tandems by the day or week from Paris à Vélo C'est Sympa (22 rue Alphonse Bourdon, 75011; tel: 01 48 87 60 01; www.parisvelosympa.com); the company also operates guided cycle tours of the city.

BUDGETING FOR YOUR TRIP

The price of accommodation varies widely. You can get a double room in a small pension for under €60 a night, or you can pay €300 in a luxury hotel. An average price, however, for an en-suite double room in a centrally located, comfortable hotel is around €100–150. Meals also cover a wide price range, but on average expect to pay around €30–40 for a three-course meal with a half-bottle of house wine. In everyday cafés and bars, a single espresso usually costs in the region of €2, and a 25cl glass of lager about €3. The average entrance price to a national museum or gallery is about €7–8 (municipal ones are free).

CAMPING

The only campsite in Paris is Camping de Paris – Bois de Boulogne (2 allée du Bord de l'Eau, 75016; tel: 01 45 24 30 00; www.camping-indigo.com), which is open all year. The site has 508 places for tents and caravans and there are 75 'cottages' for hire.

CAR HIRE (RENTAL)

To rent a car you will need your driver's licence and passport, as well as a major credit card or a large deposit. The minimum age for renting cars is 21 (but surcharges are incurred for ages 21–25), and you must have held a licence for at least a year. Third-party insurance is compulsory; full cover is recommended.

Among the international car-hire firms operating in Paris are:
Avis, tel: 08 21 23 07 60, www.avis.com.
Budget, tel: 08 25 00 35 64, www.budget.com
easyCar, tel: 01 70 61 85 52, www.easycar.com.
Europcar, tel: 08 25 35 83 58, www.europcar.com.
Hertz, tel: 01 39 38 38 38 www.hertz.com.

CLIMATE

In winter temperatures in Paris average 4°C (39°F); in summer around 22°C (72°F). Spring and autumn tend to be mild, with an average of 11°C (52°F). June, September and October are ideal for visiting, as they are warm, usually sunny, but less stifling than mid-summer.

CLOTHING

Parisians tend to be dressier than Londoners or New Yorkers. In smarter restaurants men may be expected to wear jackets, although ties are rarely insisted upon. Wear decorous clothing at religious sites.

CRIME AND SAFETY

There are pickpockets in some Métro stations and at major tourist sites. Obvious centres of prostitution (such as rue St-Denis and parts of the Bois de Boulogne) are best avoided at night. It is always a good idea to keep a photocopy of your passport in case of theft. In the event of loss or theft, you'll need to make a report at the nearest police station (*commissariat de police*), which will be required if you wish to claim on your insurance.

D

DRIVING

Driving in Paris requires confidence and concentration. Traffic drives on the right, seat belts are obligatory, and the speed limit in town is 50kph (30mph). Do not drive in bus lanes at any time, and give priority to vehicles approaching from the right. This applies to some roundabouts, where cars on the roundabout stop for those coming on to it. Most car parks are underground (see www.parkingsdeparis. com), and street parking is hard to find; spaces are usually metered Mon–Sat 9am–7pm (payment can only be made with a Paris Carte, €15 or €40 from local tabacs), and maximum stay is two hours. Fuel can be hard to find in the city centre, so if your tank is almost empty head for a *porte* (exit) on the Périphérique (the multi-lane ring road), where petrol stations are open 24 hours a day. The complete list of addresses can be found on the tourist office website (see page 129).

Drivers are liable to heavy on-the-spot fines for speeding and drink driving. The drink limit in France is 50mg/litre of alcohol in the blood (equivalent to about two glasses of wine), and is strictly enforced.

If you break down, contact Europ Assistance (tel: 01 41 85 86 86), but expect to pay a high cost unless you have already taken out its insurance cover (www.europ-assistance.co.uk). Other 24-hour breakdown services include Action Auto Assistance (tel: 08 00 00 80 00).

driver's licence **permis de conduire**
car registration papers **carte grise**
Yield to traffic from right **Priorité à droite**
Slow down **Ralentir**
Keep right/left **Serrez à droite/à gauche**
One way **Sens unique**
Give way **Cédez la priorité/le passage**

E

ELECTRICITY
You'll need an adapter: French sockets have two round holes. Supplies are 220 volt, and US equipment will need a transformer.

EMBASSIES AND CONSULATES
Australia 4 rue Jean-Rey, 75015; tel: 01 40 59 33 00; www.france.embassy.gov.au

Canada 35 avenue Montaigne, 75008; tel: 01 44 43 29 00; www.amb-canada.fr

New Zealand 103 rue de Grenelle, 75007; tel: 01 45 01 43 43; www.nzembassy.com/france

Republic of Ireland Embassy: 12 avenue Foch, 75016; tel: 01 44 17 67 00. Consulate: 4 rue Rude, 75016; tel: 01 44 17 67 00; www.embassyofireland.fr

South Africa 59 quai d'Orsay, 75007; tel: 01 53 59 23 23; www.afriquesud.net

UK Embassy: 35 rue du Faubourg-St-Honoré, 75008; tel: 01 44 51 31 00; www.amb-grandebretagne.fr. Consulate: 16 rue d'Anjou, 75008; tel: 01 44 51 31 00

US Embassy: 2 avenue Gabriel, 75008; tel: 01 43 12 22 22; http://france.usembassy.gov. Consulate: 4 avenue Gabriel, 75008

EMERGENCIES
Ambulance (SAMU) 15
Police *(police secours)* 17
Fire brigade *(sapeurs-pompiers)* 18
From a mobile phone: 112

Fire! **Au feu!**
Help! **Au secours!**

G

GAY AND LESBIAN TRAVELLERS

The city has a large, visible and quite relaxed gay community. Gay bars and clubs are concentrated in the Marais. The magazine *Têtu*, available at kiosks, is a useful source of information (in French) as is www.paris-gay.com (in English).

GETTING THERE (see also Airports)

By Air: Air France is the main agent for flights to France from the US and within Europe and also handles bookings for some of the smaller operators, such as Brit Air. For British travellers, operators such as British Airways (www.ba.com) and the low-cost airlines easyJet (www.easyjet.com), Flybe (www.flybe.com) and Jet2 (www.jet2.com) offer flights to Paris from London and other British cities. See www.skyscanner.net to compare prices.

By Rail: The Eurostar is the most convenient way to get to Paris (Gare du Nord) from the UK, with fast, frequent rail services from London (St Pancras International), Ebbsfleet and Ashford. The service runs about 12 times a day and takes two and a quarter hours (two hours from Ebbsfleet). For reservations, contact Eurostar on tel: 0843 218 6186 (UK) or 08 92 35 35 39 (France), or visit www.eurostar.com. There are reduced fares for children aged 4–11; children under three travel free but are not guaranteed a seat.

By Car: Eurotunnel takes cars and passengers from Folkestone to Calais on Le Shuttle. It takes 35 minutes from platform to platform and about one hour from motorway to motorway. You can book in advance with Eurotunnel on tel: 0844 335 3535 (UK) or 08 10 63 03 04 (France) or at www.eurotunnel.com or just turn up and take the next available service. Le Shuttle runs 24 hours a day, all year, and there are between two and five an hour.

By Bus: National Express subsidiary Eurolines runs daily services from London (Victoria Coach Station) to Paris (Métro Gallieni), providing one of the cheaper ways to get there. For more information, tel: 0871 781 8178 (UK) or 08 92 89 90 91 (France), or visit www.eurolines.co.uk.

GUIDES AND TOURS

Find multilingual guides and interpreters through the tourist office (see page 129). One of the best suppliers of guided tours is Paris Walks, which has been going for nearly 20 years; see www.paris-walks.com. To save shoe leather, try a tour on a Segway, a motorised scooter-style vehicle; see http://paris.citysegwaytours.com for more details.

H

HEALTH AND MEDICAL CARE (see also Emergencies)

EU Nationals: EU nationals can receive emergency medical treatment. You will have to pay, but can claim from the French Sécurité Sociale, which refunds up to 70 per cent of your medical bill. You must have a European Health Insurance Card (www.ehic.org.uk).

North American Citizens: Contact the International Association for Medical Assistance to Travellers (iamat), tel: 416 652 0137 (Canada) or 716 754 4883 (US), www.iamat.org. This non-profit group offers members fixed rates for medical treatment from participating physicians. Membership is free, but a donation is requested.

English-speaking health services are at the American Hospital, tel: 01 46 41 25 25, www.american-hospital.org, and the Hertford British Hospital, tel: 0147 59 59 59, www.british-hospital.org.

Chemists: Pharmacies can be identified by their green (usually neon-lit) 'plus' sign. Pharmacie des Halles (10 boulevard de Sébastopol, 75004; Métro Châtelet; tel: 01 42 72 03 23) is open 9am–midnight, Mon-Sat, and 9am–10pm on Sun. Publicis Drugstore (133 avenue des Champs-Élysées, 75008; Métro Etoile; tel: 01 47 20 39 25) is open 24 hours daily.

L

LOST PROPERTY

If you lose your passport, report it to your consulate (see page 122 orsearch for 'Ambassades et Consulats' on www.pagesjaunes.fr).

If your credit card is lost or stolen, the numbers to ring are:

American Express, tel: 01 47 77 72 00
Mastercard, tel: 08 00 90 13 87
Visa, tel: 08 00 90 11 79

To reclaim anything else you have lost, you should go (with ID) to the Bureau des Objets Trouvés (36 rue des Morillons, 75732 Cedex 15; Métro Convention; tel: 08 21 00 25 25; open weekdays 8.30am–5pm, except Fri, when it shuts at 4.30pm). You need to visit the office in person, as no information is given over the telephone.

M

MAPS

Paris Pratique par Arrondissement, an indexed, pocket-sized street atlas, is the most useful map for visitors. It can be bought for around €6 at newsstands and kiosks. Most Métro stations supply free, decent maps of the Métro system, bus network and RER train system.

MEDIA

Newspapers: The two main national dailies are *Le Monde*, which has a leftish slant, and the more conservative *Le Figaro*. The local daily is *Le Parisien*. British, American and other European dailies are widely available on the same day at city-centre kiosks and shops showing 'journaux' or 'presse' signs. The US-flavoured FUSAC (www.fusac.fr) is a free fortnightly English-language magazine containing job offers, classified ads and some event information; it is available in Anglo-themed bars and restaurants.

Radio: France Inter (87.8 MHz) is the main national radio station, with a lot of serious discussion. RTL (104.3 MHz) is the most popular station throughout France, playing music from the charts, interspersed with chat shows.

Television: TF1, France 2, France 3, Canal+, France 5/Arte and M6 are the six main television stations on offer.

MONEY

Currency: The euro (€) is divided into 100 cents (¢ or ct). Coins *(pièces)* come in 1, 2, 5, 10, 20 and 50 cents, and 1 and 2 euros. Banknotes *(billets)* come in 5, 10, 20, 50, 100, 200 and 500 euros. ATMs are widespread, and accept most of the major international debit and credit cards; check withdrawal charges with your bank before you go. Some cards, including Halifax and Saga, don't charge fees for use abroad.

Banks and currency exchange offices (banque; bureau de change): Take your passport when changing money or travellers' cheques. Your hotel may offer an exchange service, though at a worse rate.

Travellers' cheques: These are widely accepted (with identification).

I want to change some pounds/dollars **Je voudrais changer des livres sterling/dollars**
Do you accept travellers' cheques/this credit card? **Acceptez-vous les chèques de voyage/cette carte de crédit?**

O

OPENING HOURS

Traditionally, banks open Mon–Fri 9am–5pm and close at the weekend, though many now open on Saturday morning and close on Monday. Food shops tend to open early. Traditionally, most shops close for lunch, but in Paris, many remain open, closing at 7 or 7.30pm. The larger department stores do not close at lunchtime and are open until 9 or 10pm on Thursday. Most shops close on Sunday; many museums close on Monday or Tuesday and ticket offices usually shut at least 30 minutes prior to the official closing time.

P

POLICE (see also Emergencies)

The blue-uniformed police who keep law and order and direct traffic are, as a general rule, courteous and helpful to visitors. The CRS (Compagnies républicaines de sécurité) are the tough guys, brought in for demonstrations. The main police station is the Préfecture de Police, at 9 boulevard du Palais on the Ile-de-la-Cité (tel: 01 53 73 53 73; www.prefecture-police-paris.interieur.gouv.fr).

If you need to call for police help, dial 17 (anywhere in France).

Where is the nearest police station? **Où se trouve le commissariat de police le plus proche?**

POST OFFICES

The French postal service is run by La Poste (www.laposte.fr). Main post offices are open Mon–Fri 8am–8pm, Sat 9am–1pm. The central post office (52 rue du Louvre, 75001; tel: 36 31) operates a 24-hour service. Stamps (timbres) are available at most tobacconists (tabacs). Post boxes are yellow.

PUBLIC HOLIDAYS

Public offices, banks and most shops close on public holidays, though you will find the odd corner shop open.

1 January Jour de l'An New Year's Day
1 May Fête du Travail Labour Day
8 May Fête de la Victoire Victory Day (1945)
14 July Fête Nationale Bastille Day
15 August Assomption Assumption

1 November *Toussaint* All Saints' Day
11 November *Armistice* Armistice Day (1918)
25 December *Noël* Christmas Day
Moveable dates:
Pâques Easter
Lundi de Pâques Easter Monday
Ascension Ascension Day
Lundi de Pentecôte Whit Monday

T

TELEPHONES

Telephone numbers in France have 10 digits. Paris and Île de France numbers begin with 01; toll-free phone numbers begin with 0800; other numbers beginning with 08 are charged at variable rates; 06 numbers are mobile numbers. There are coin-operated (rare) and card-operated phone boxes in Paris. You get 50 percent more call time for your money if you ring between 10.30pm and 8am on weekdays, and from 2pm at weekends. A *télécarte* can be bought at various prices from kiosks, tabacs and post offices. You can also dial from all post offices. Cafés and tabacs often have public phones.

UK mobile phones will work in Paris; ask your network provider if your phone is set up for international roaming and consider buying bundles of minutes to keep your call costs down. For long stays, you can buy a pay-as-you-go *(sans abonnement)* mobile phone from Orange (www.orange.fr), SFR (www.sfr.fr) or Bouygues Telecom (www.bouyguestelecom.fr), all of whom have shops on French high streets.

Direct Dialling to Paris from the UK: 00 (international code) + 33 (France) + 1 (Paris) + an eight-figure number. To call abroad from France, dial the international access code (00), then the country code.
Directory Enquiries: 118700 (France Télécom), 118222 or 118000; for a full list of 118 numbers see www.appel118.fr.
Operator: 3123

TIME DIFFERENCES

France keeps to Central European Time (GMT +1 hour; GMT +2 hours Apr-Oct). When it is noon in Paris, it is 11am in London, 6am in New York, 10pm in Auckland, 8pm in Sydney and noon in Johannesburg.

What time is it? **Quelle heure est-il?**

TIPPING

By law, restaurant bills must include the service charge, usually 12 or 15 percent. Nevertheless, it is common to leave a small additional tip (around 5 per cent) for the waiter, if the service has been good. With taxis, it is usual to round up to the nearest euro.

TOILETS

There are some 400 automated public toilets (sanisettes) parked on pavements across the city; all are clearly marked. They are unisex, disinfected after each use, and free of charge. Most cafés have toilets, although these are, in principle, reserved for their customers.

TOURIST INFORMATION

The main Paris tourism authority is the Office du Tourisme de Paris, tel: 08 92 68 30 00, www.parisinfo.com. Branches are listed below.
In the UK: ATOUT France, 300 High Holborn, London WC1V 7JHL, tel: 0906 824 4123 (calls cost 60p per minute), www.franceguide.com.
In the US: ATOUT France, 825 Third Avenue, 29th floor, NY-10022; tel: 212 745 0952, http://us.franceguide.com.
In Canada: 1800 avenue McGill Collège, Bureau 1010, Montréal, Québec, H3A 3J6; tel: 514 288 2026; http://ca.rendezvousenfrance.com.
In Australia: French Tourist Bureau, Level 13, 25 Bligh Street, 2000 NSW, Sydney; tel: 9231 5244; http://au.franceguide.com.
In Paris: Pyramides: 25 rue des Pyramides, 75001. Daily 9am–7pm (from 10am Nov–Apr). Gare du Nord: 18 rue de Dunkerque, 75010.

Daily 8am–6pm. Gare de Lyon: 20 boulevard Diderot, 75012. Mon–Sat 8am–6pm. Gare de l'Est: place du 11 novembre 1918, 75010. Mon–Sat 8am–7pm. Anvers: 72 boulevard de Rochechouart, 75018. Daily 10am–6pm.

TRANSPORT

All public transport in Paris is run by the Régie Autonome des Transports Parisiens (RATP; tel: 32 46; www.ratp.fr). There is an information office at 54 quai de la Rapée, 75012 Paris.

Bus (autobus): Bus transport around Paris is efficient, though not always fast. You can obtain a bus route plan from Métro station ticket counters. Most buses run 7am–8.30pm, some until 12.30am. Service is reduced on Sundays and public holidays. Special Noctilien services (www.noctilien.fr) operate on over 45 routes across the capital and suburbs, from 12.30am–5.30am every hour, with Châtelet as the hub.

Bus journeys take one ticket. You can buy a ticket as you board, but it is cheaper to buy a book of tickets *(carnet)* from any Métro station or tobacconist. Punch your ticket in the validating machine when you get on. You can also buy special one-, three- or five-day tourist passes or the weekly ticket and Navigo *(see below)*. Show these special tickets to the driver as you get on, rather than putting them in the punching machine. The fine for being caught without a ticket is €5 (or €30 for deferred payment).

Métro: The Paris Métropolitain ('Métro') is fast, efficient and inexpensive. You get 10 journeys (including connections) for the price of seven with a *carnet* (book) of tickets. Tickets are also valid for the bus network and for the RER (in zones 1-2). Keep your ticket until you exit the station. A special ticket called **Paris Visite**, valid for one, three or five days, allows unlimited travel on the bus or Métro, and reductions on entrance fees to various attractions. A day ticket, **Mobilis**, is valid for the Métro, RER, buses, suburban trains and some airport buses. For longer stays, the best buy is a **Navigo** smart card, valid for unlimited rides inside Paris on the Métro and bus, either weekly *(heb-*

domadaire) Mon–Sun, monthly *(mensuel)*, or annual *(annuel)*. Have a passport photo ready.

Métro stations have big, easy-to-read maps. Services start at 5.30am and finish around 1am (last trains leave end stations at 12.30am).

Train: The SNCF (French railway authority) is fast, comfortable and efficient. The **high-speed service** (TGV) is excellent but more expensive (www.sncf.com or www.voyages-sncf.com). Make sure you validate *(composter)* your train ticket before boarding by inserting it in one of the orange machines on the way to the platform.

Taxi: Taxis are generally reasonably priced, though there are extra charges for putting luggage in the boot and for pick-up at a station or airport. Taxi drivers can refuse to carry more than three passengers. The fourth, when admitted, pays a supplement.

You will find taxis cruising around or at stands all over the city, but finding an empty one can take a long time, especially at busy times of day. You can recognise an unoccupied cab by an illuminated sign on its roof. Fares differ according to the zones covered or the time of the day (you'll be charged more between 7pm and 7am and on Sunday). A fare between Roissy-Charles-de-Gaulle Airport and central Paris might be as much as €50 by day, €60 at night.

The following taxi companies take phone bookings 24 hours a day:

Alpha: 01 45 85 85 85

G7: 36 07

Taxis Bleus: 36 09

TRAVELLERS WITH DISABILITIES

Wheelchairs are available to rent from **CRF Matériel Médical**, 153 boulevard Voltaire, 75011, tel: 01 43 73 98 98. **Ptitcar**, www.ptitcar. com, has a fleet of wheelchair-accessible vehicles for transport and tours; they also prepare holiday itineraries for wheelchair users. Wheelchair users can visit Paris on Wheels, www.parisonwheels. com, for guided tours tailored to disabled visitors.

Useful Organisations
France: Association des Paralysés de France, Service Information, 13 place de Rungis, 75013; tel: 0153 80 92 97; www.apf.asso.fr.
UK: Disability Rights UK, 12 City Forum, 250 City Road, London EC1V 8AF; tel: 020 7250 3222; www.disabilityrightsuk.org.
US: Society for Accessible Travel and Hospitality (SATH), 347 Fifth Ave., Suite 605, New York, NY 10016; tel: 212 447 7284; www.sath.org.

V

VISAS AND ENTRY REQUIREMENTS
Nationals of EU countries need a valid passport or identity document to enter France. Nationals from Australia, Canada, New Zealand and the US need passports; South African nationals need a visa: contact Consulat de France, Standard Bank Building, 3rd Floor, 191 Jan Smuts Avenue, Cnr 7th Avenue, Parktown North 2196, Johannesburg; tel: 011 778 56 18; www.consulfrance-jhb.org.

W

WEBSITES
www.monuments-nationaux.fr Guide to national monuments
www.paris.fr General information on Paris from the city council
www.parisvoice.com Online magazine about Paris for English speakers

Y

YOUTH HOSTELS
A free guide to French youth hostels is available from the Fédération Unie des Auberges de Jeunesse (FUAJ), 27 rue Pajol, 75018 Paris; tel: 01 44 89 87 27; www.fuaj.org. Tourist information offices provide a booklet entitled *Jeunes à Paris* (Young People in Paris), listing details of hostels, student halls and other types of low-budget accommodation.

This list is divided geographically, covering hotels on the islands and the Right and Left banks. Note that the numbers in the post-code indicate the *arrondissement* (district), so 75004 is the 4th *arrondissement*.

Hotels on the islands are mainly small and old-fashioned, and few have lifts. Around the Louvre and Tuileries are some of the city's star addresses, such as the Ritz; further north, on and around the Grands Boulevards, are unassuming establishments with modern amenities. Try Beaubourg, Marais or Bastille for a crop of modern boutique hotels.

Western Paris offers full-on luxury. Montmartre hotels, on the other hand, tend to capitalise on the Butte's romantic reputation, but often nakedly angle their rates at the tourist crowd.

On the Left Bank, the Latin Quarter and St-Germain-des-Prés have chic, elegant and traditional establishments, but staying here is rarely cheap. You almost always pay a premium around the Eiffel Tower too. There are a few pleasant addresses to be found in Montparnasse.

The following ranges give an idea of the price for an en-suite double room per night. Service and tax are included; generally, breakfast is not.

€€€€	over 300 euros
€€€	200–300 euros
€€	100–200 euros
€	55–100 euros

THE ISLANDS

Hôtel des Deux-Îles €€€ *59 rue St-Louis-en-l'Île, 75004; tel: 01 43 26 13 35;* www.deuxiles-paris-hotel.com. Set in a small and attractive 17th-century mansion on the main street of the tranquil Île St-Louis, this hotel, with just 17 rooms, is comfortable and friendly, with a cellar bar and a vaulted breakfast room with stone walls. Rooms are compact but nicely decorated. Wi-fi.

Hôtel du Jeu de Paume €€€€ *54 rue St-Louis-en-l'Île, 75004; tel: 01 43 26 14 18*; www.jeudepaumehotel.com. This 30-room Île St-Louis hotel is decorated in chic contemporary style, but has kept its 17th century *jeu de paume* (real-tennis) court. Wi-fi.

Hôtel de Lutèce €€€ *65 rue St-Louis-en-l'Île, 75004; tel: 01 43 26 23 52*; www.paris-hotel-lutece.com. This lovely Île St-Louis hotel is under the same management as the Deux-Îles (see page 133). It has 23 tiny, attractive and quiet rooms, several with exposed wooden beams. Those on the sixth floor are the most romantic. Wi-fi.

LOUVRE AND TUILERIES

Hôtel Costes €€€€ *239 rue St-Honoré, 75001; tel: 01 42 44 50 00*; www.hotelcostes.com. This super-hip hotel is just off elegant place Vendôme in an exclusive neighbourhood lined with chic boutiques. The rooms are exquisitely decorated with Baroque paintings, heavy drapes and antiques. Some bathrooms have claw-foot bathtubs and mosaic tiles. Owner Jean-Louis Costes dislikes artificial light, so the hallways are lit with candles; even the beautiful indoor pool is dark.

Grand Hotel du Palais Royal €€€€ *4 rue de Valois, 75001; tel: 01 42 96 15 35*; www.grandhoteldupalaisroyal.com. In an 18th century building in the south eastern corner of the elegant Palais Royal is this intimate luxury hotel, which opened its doors in the summer of 2013. The 68 rooms and suites, some with their own balcony, successfully marry classical style with contemporary lines. As well as a restaurant and bar, there is also a spa, which uses Carita products.

Hôtel Mansart €€€ *5 rue des Capucines, 75001; tel: 01 42 61 50 28*; www.paris-hotel-mansart.com. With some of the 57 rooms overlooking place Vendôme, this four-star hotel, named after the architect of Versailles, is a bargain for this area. Rooms are decorated in traditional style, furnished with antiques, yet have a contemporary feel and there is a lovely stained glass window in the breakfast room. The hotel has been completely refurbished.

THE GRANDS BOULEVARDS

Buddha Bar Hotel €€€€ *4 rue d'Anjou, 75008; tel: 01 83 96 88 88;* www. buddhabarhotelparis.com. A couple of streets west of place de la Madeleine, this ultra-hip hotel opened its doors in the summer of 2013. The 18th-century building is decorated in neo-Asian style, the food is Asian-Fusion and the Quatre cocktail bar is fast becoming the place to be seen.

Hôtel Chopin € *46 passage Jouffroy, 75009; tel: 01 47 70 58 10;* www. hotelchopin.fr. Set at the end of a historic 19th-century glass-and-steel-roofed arcade, this is a quiet, friendly, simply furnished hotel. It is popular, too, so book well in advance.

Hôtel Langlois €€ *63 rue St-Lazare, 75009; tel: 01 48 74 78 24;* www. hotel-langlois.com. If you fancy stepping back in time then this three-star hotel is the place for you. Rooms are decorated in Belle Epoque and Art Nouveau style, each furnished with antiques and paintings, each with original features dating from 1870 when the building was constructed. Breakfast isn't cheap (€13) but it's worth trying to check out the old-fashioned birdcage in the breakfast room.

W Paris – Opéra €€€€ *4 rue Meyerbeer, 75009; tel: 01 77 48 94 94;* www.wparisopera.com. In a grand 1870s building near the Opéra, this is the place to come if comfort is as important as style: the hotel is famous for its beds (the two Extreme Wow Suites have circular ones) and Egyptian cotton linen. All rooms have 40" TVs, rainforest showers and iPod docking stations. Chill out to the DJs in the W Lounge or try some gourmet food in the Coquette restaurant.

BEAUBOURG, MARAIS AND BASTILLE

Hôtel Bourg Tibourg €€€ *19 rue du Bourg-Tibourg, 75004; tel: 01 42 78 47 39;* www.bourgtibourg.com. Situated on a charming narrow street in the heart of the Marais, this 17th-century building is home to a well-kept, affordable boutique hotel stylishly decorated by celebrity designer Jacques Garcia in reds, blacks and Moorish blues and golds. Breakfast is served in a vaulted dining room with exposed stone.

Le Citizen Hotel du Canal €€€ *96 quai de Jemmapes, 75010 tel: 01 83 62 55 50*; www.lecitizenhotel.com. In a lovely location next to the Canal St-Martin, this eco-friendly, modern hotel has just 12 rooms, including two suites, with all mod cons including an iPad. There are regular art exhibitions and breakfast is included in the room price.

Hôtel Duo €€€ *11 rue du Temple, 75004; tel: 01 42 72 72 22*; www.duo-paris.com. This trendy hotel has an excellent location in the Marais. Rooms are furnished in contemporary style, with good-sized bathrooms. There is a bar downstairs, a courtyard garden and a gym.

Mama Shelter €€ *109 rue de Bagnolet, 75020; tel: 01 43 48 48 48*; www.mamashelter.com. This 170-room hotel has won a slew of awards for its looks, facilities, and value. The location is a fair distance east of Bastille, but the sleek Philippe Starck-designed rooms all come with iMacs, microwaves and free movies. Mama regularly hosts DJ sessions, yet has also been voted best business hotel in Europe two years running.

Pavillon de la Reine €€€€ *28 place des Vosges, 75003; tel: 01 40 29 19 19*; www.pavillon-de-la-reine.com. This romantic, stylish hotel, located on the beautiful place des Vosges, feels like a country château. Rooms vary greatly in size and price, but most have four-poster beds, exposed wooden beams and antiques. There is also a cosy lobby bar with evening wine-tasting, a spa, and manicured gardens.

WESTERN PARIS

Le Dokhan's Hotel €€€€ *117 rue de Lauriston, 75016; tel: 01 53 65 66 99*; www.radissonblu.com. This hotel in the Radisson Blu chain has a fine western location with good views of the Eiffel Tower. The decor is classic luxury with contemporary touches: high ceilings, lots of wood and old-style fittings all set off by modern colours and warm lighting. There is a stylish champagne bar but no restaurant.

Saint James Paris €€€€ *43 avenue Bugeaud, 75016; tel: 01 44 05 81 81*; www.saint-james-paris.com. This outrageously luxurious mansion near Étoile was done out in 2011 by British interior designer Bambi Sloan in a sort of modern Baroque, complete with chandeliers. Among other glories, there is a drop-dead gorgeous library bar and a large garden dotted with kiosks made to look like Montgolfier balloons – whose real, historic predecessors used to take off here.

MONTMARTRE

Chat Noir Design Hôtel €€ *68 boulevard de Clichy, 75018; tel: 01 42 64 15 26*; www.hotel-chatnoir-paris.com. The ubiquitous black cat image gives away this hotel location in the former famous nightclub of the same name. Rooms are white, bright and contemporary with splashes of red, black and yellow. The area is a racy one.

Hôtel Ermitage €€ *24 rue Lamarck, 75018; tel: 01 42 64 79 22*; www. ermitagesacrecoeur.fr. This 12-room hotel is located close to Sacré-Cœur in an old residential neighbourhood. It is a good budget choice, with friendly staff and colourful bedrooms decorated in French farmhouse style. There is a lovely courtyard and terrace, where breakfast (included in the price) is served in summer. No credit cards.

Terrass Hotel €€€ *12–14 rue Joseph de Maistre, 75018; tel: 01 46 06 72 85*; www.terrass-hotel.com. This renovated Montmartre hotel has one considerable advantage over its rivals, in addition to its stylish decor and chic piano bar: the open-air lounge on its roof. Drinks and meals are served here in good weather, with panoramic views of the capital.

LATIN QUARTER AND ST-GERMAIN-DES-PRÉS

Abbaye St-Germain €€€€ *10 rue Cassette, 75006; tel: 01 45 44 38 11*; www.hotelabbayeparis.com. This 17th century abbey, attractively situated between the Jardin du Luxembourg and St-Germain-des-Prés, has been beautifully adapted into a hotel. A favourite haunt of writers and artists, the charm of the old decor has been maintained – some of the 46 rooms have beams – but there are all mod cons, and a lovely garden. Staff are helpful and attentive.

Hôtel d'Angleterre €€€ *44 rue Jacob, 75006; tel: 01 42 60 34 72*; www.hotel-dangleterre.com. The location could not be better, on a quiet, upmarket street lined with art galleries. This lovely hotel was the site at which the Treaty of Paris, proclaiming the independence of the US, was signed in 1783; in the 19th century it was used as the British Embassy. Ernest Hemingway lodged here (in room 14) in 1921. Rooms are fairly small and furnished with antiques; only the top-floor doubles are spacious. Delightful terrace and garden.

Hôtel Familia €€ *11 rue des Ecoles, 75005; tel: 01 43 54 55 27;* www. hotel-paris-familia.com. Within a few minutes' walk of the islands and St-Germain-des-Prés, the Familia offers solid comforts in small-ish rooms for a modest price; rooms on the fifth and sixth floors have views of Notre-Dame. Another attraction for the hotel's many regular guests is the hospitable Gaucheron family who live on the premises and take pride in every detail.

Hôtel des Grandes Ecoles €€ *75 rue du Cardinal-Lemoine, 75005; tel: 01 43 26 79 23;* www.hotel-grandes-ecoles.com. At first glance, you might think you were in the French countryside. There are 51 large, prettily furnished rooms around a cobbled courtyard and garden of established trees and trellised roses. Although it is a short uphill walk from the Métro, you are still near enough to attractions including rue Mouffetard. No TVs.

Hôtel de Nesle €€ *7 rue de Nesle, 75006; tel: 01 43 54 62 41;* www. hoteldenesleparis.com. A laid-back students' and backpackers' hotel. Facilities are basic, but bedrooms are cheerfully decorated with murals, furnished to various eclectic themes and spotless. There is also a garden with a pond and an impressive palm tree.

Hotel Le Six €€€ *14 rue Stanislas, 75006; tel: 01 42 22 00 75;* www. hotel-le-six.com. Design-conscious but child-friendly boutique hotel, where the rooms have iPod/iPhone docks, Nespresso machines and L'Occitane toiletries. Relax with a drink in the glass-roofed lounge, book a private yoga class in the fitness centre or ease away aches and pains in the hammam. No restaurant.

AROUND THE EIFFEL TOWER

Amélie €€ *5 rue Amélie, 75007; tel: 01 45 51 74 75;* www.hotelamelie-paris.com. A short walk from the Eiffel Tower, this small, friendly, family-run hotel has some of the lowest rates in the area. Renovated rooms have small refrigerators and private bathrooms. A narrow wooden staircase leads up to the four levels of rooms; there is no lift. Breakfast is served in the small lobby.

Hôtel Lenox €€€ *9 rue de l'Université, 75007; tel: 01 42 96 10 95;* www.hotel-lenox-st-germain-paris.com. This trendy hotel is decorated in Art Deco style and is very popular among style-conscious types. There is a bar and the rooms are spotless. Reserve well in advance.

Hôtel Verneuil €€€ *8 rue de Verneuil, 75007; tel: 01 42 60 82 14;* www.hotel-verneuil-saint-germain.com. Lovely hotel in an elegant 17th century building in the upmarket 7th arrondissement, with small but attractive rooms renovated in contemporary style. Discreet service. Singer Serge Gainsbourg lived on this street, and the wall outside his old house is decorated with graffiti in homage. Well placed for St-Germain.

MONTPARNASSE

Hôtel Ariane €€ *35 rue de la Sablière, 75014; tel: 01 45 45 67 13;* www.hotel-ariane.fr. Peace and quiet is one of the Ariane's biggest selling points. Its 30 rooms have been renovated, each with its own take on the theme of 'Time' – hourglasses, and so on. All have free Wi-fi and flat-screen TV.

Hôtel Istria €€ *29 rue Campagne Première, 75014; tel: 01 43 20 91 82;* www.hotel-istria-paris.com. Three star hotel, whose exotic previous guests have included Man Ray, Eric Satie and Rainer Maria Rilker. The 26 renovated rooms are based around an attractive interior courtyard; all have flat-screen TVs and Wi-fi.

INDEX

INSIGHT ⊙ GUIDES POCKET GUIDE

PARIS

First Edition 2016
Written by Martin Gostelow & Simon Cropper
Updated by Magdalena Helsztyńska-Stadnik
Update Production: AM Services
Edited by Kate Drynan
Maps updated by Carte Warsaw
Photography credits: AKG 21; Britta Jaschinski/Apa Publications 40, 79; Dreamstime 24, 86; Getty 14; Ilpo Musto/Apa Publications 2/3T, 2/3M, 4ML, 4TL, 6TL, 26, 28/29, 46, 51, 52, 54, 64, 75, 97; iStockphoto 18, 34/35, 88; Kevin Cummins/Apa Publications 2TL, 3MC, 4ML, 6ML, 10/11, 28,38, 39, 42, 44/45, 50, 60/61, 66, 68, 69, 70, 82/83; Ming Tang-Evans/Apa Publications 2BL, 2TC, 2MC, 2/3T, 2/3M, 3MC, 4MR, 4TL, 4/5M, 5MC, 4/5T, 5TC, 6ML, 7MC, 7MC, 7TC, 13, 17, 30, 30/31, 32/33, 36/37, 48, 49, 57, 59, 62, 72, 73, 76/77, 80, 81, 84/85, 90, 92, 94, 98, 100/101, 102, 104/105, 106; Sylvaine Poitau/Apa Publications 22
Cover picture: iStock

All Rights Reserved
© 2016 Apa Digital (CH) AG and Apa Publications (UK) Ltd

Distribution
UK, Ireland and Europe: Apa Publications (UK) Ltd; sales@insightguides.com
United States and Canada: Ingram Publisher Services; ips@ingramcontent.com

Australia and New Zealand: Woodslane; info@woodslane.com.au
Southeast Asia: Apa Publications (SN) Pte; singaporeoffice@insightguides.com
Hong Kong, Taiwan and China: Apa Publications (HK) Ltd; hongkongoffice@insightguides.com
Worldwide: Apa Publications (UK) Ltd; sales@insightguides.com

Special Sales, Content Licensing and CoPublishing
Insight Guides can be purchased in bulk quantities at discounted prices. We can create special editions, personalised jackets and corporate imprints tailored to your needs. sales@insightguides.com; www.insightguides.biz

Printed in Poland

No part of this book may be reproduced, stored in a retrieval system or transmitted in any form or means electronic, mechanical, photocopying, recording or otherwise, without prior written permission from Apa Publications.

Contact us
Every effort has been made to provide accurate information in this publication, but changes are inevitable. The publisher cannot be responsible for any resulting loss, inconvenience or injury. We would appreciate it if readers would call our attention to any errors or outdated information. We also welcome your suggestions; please contact us at: hello@insightguides.com www.insightguides.com

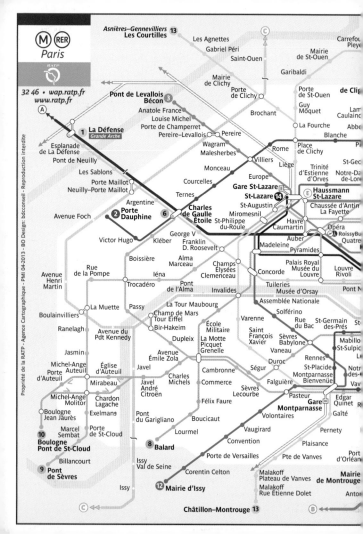